UN TETHERED

Nathan James Thomas bought a ticket for 20,000 kilometres on the Greyhound Bus network in Australia when he was seventeen years old. Over the next decade, he lived in China, Spain, Poland and Hungary, visiting and experiencing dozens of other countries along the way. In 2014, Nathan founded the digital travel magazine *Intrepid Times* as a vehicle for sharing stories from the road and as an excuse to meet and interview his favourite writers. It has since grown into a thriving global community of thousands of writers and travellers. His own travel writing has been published in places like *Lonely Planet, Roads and Kingdoms* and *Outpost Magazine*. With his two previous books, *Fearless Footsteps* and *Travel Your Way*, Nathan presents a vision of travel that is both challenging and humbling, an experience not of finding yourself, but of losing yourself.

UNTETHERED

Living the digital nomad life
in an uncertain world

Nathan James Thomas

EXISLE
PUBLISHING

First published 2023

Exisle Publishing Pty Ltd
PO Box 864, Chatswood, NSW 2057, Australia
226 High Street, Dunedin, 9016, New Zealand
www.exislepublishing.com

A CiP record for this book is available from the National Library of Australia.

ISBN 978-1-922539-69-4

Designed by Enni Tuomisalo
Typeset in PT Serif, 11pt
Printed by Sheridan

This book uses paper sourced under ISO 14001 guidelines from well-managed forests and other controlled sources.

10 9 8 7 6 5 4 3 2 1

Disclaimer

While this book is intended as a general information resource and all care has been taken in compiling the contents, neither the author nor the publisher and their distributors can be held responsible for any loss, claim or action that may arise from reliance on the information contained in this book.

To anyone reading this book far from home,
longing for the journey to continue …

Contents

Foreword

~~~

The first person who ever saw you slapped you until you screamed.

You don't remember it, but *that* was your introduction to existence: shock. Pain. Noise. Love. The world is wide and wild, and that is how you enter it — by sliding, headfirst, into its all, the very sweat of it: the stun of light, the thrill of breath, the surprise of violence, the warmth of a mother's arms.

And that is just the very first of many, many things you won't remember.

The world is full of people with boxes. People who live in a little box and ride in a little box to work in a little box in order to make money to pay for the little box they live in and the little box they ride in and all the little boxes they buy to give to other people and keep for themselves. This makes sense; boxes are easy. Boxes are the easiest form of life. Boxes are the easiest place to be someone else if that is all you know how to be — if you have already forgotten, as so many of us do, the feral animal you are. The feral animal who entered this one and precious life screaming, seeing for the first time, surrounded by light and love. Boxes are the easiest thing to forget.

There's a challenging reality that most folks do not confront, but should: this is all there is. Your computer, once its battery runs out, does not remember anything that happened to it. You, too, run on a computer. One day the electricity will run out. You won't remember any of this: not that slow-cooked duck in Montreal, nor the carts in Cambodia, or the girl in Italy. You won't recall the tastes you savoured, the aromas you breathed in so deeply they inhabited you forever, or the bodies — ugh, the sweat of it — that rose and fell above you, beneath you.

This is a reason to rejoice. The worst things in your life never even happened. Every mistake, every missed opportunity, will one day wash away like a teardrop in the ocean. Instead, you get this: an invitation to one and precious life. You get a reprieve from boxes. Nobody in this world has ever found happiness by waiting for paradise to arrive to them; you need, instead, to go find it. And it's hard to get to. If it were easy, everybody would do it.

You get to become untethered.

It's not a natural realization; after all, we all forget how we began. For everyone it's different, but for me it was a gift — not the kind you buy in little boxes, but the kind the wide and wild world hands out so often and so naturally: when I was a boy, my mother died. It's a horrible event in any life — made luckier only by the fact that I won't remember it — but it was unquestionably the finest gift she ever gave me. I learned, at a very early age, how finite this is and we are. Our family was of meagre fortune in those days and these alike; we'd had an old, small television propped up in our kitchen that got five channels, and we only seemed to ever watch old movies still broadcast in monochrome. Watching men with grey faces kiss women with grey faces in worlds of grey soil and grey skies, I didn't understand that it wasn't a change in the atmosphere, but in technology: I asked my grandmother if, in fact, the world had once been totally lacking in colour.

She proceeded to tell me about the gardens she grew up in, singing (in her way) our natural anthem: she told me about all the things a century earlier that bloomed and flourished, almost too many to count. Green grass, yellow forsythia, magenta azaleas, pink cherry blossoms, blue-bells, orange tulips, red-breasted robins. The world was always in colour; the only thing in black and white was that little box.

Since then, I've always been leaving, not out of my life but *into* it. For me, it's always been travel — I've been on the road most of my adult life — and with good reason. Almost everybody on Earth lives outside my apartment, and all of them have something to teach me. I've made so many mistakes, and found so many joys. But my mistakes and joys are temporary, and seem to grow larger each and every morning that the sun rises and I do, too. But there's still a challenging reality to confront: you do not accident into life. You are invited to it. And, invited to life, you must seize upon that opportunity.

It is okay to be a little reckless before you are wrecked, to be one of the sailors and lovers who press their bows against the breakers. They need wilder, cruder waves; they sicken of the calm who knew the storm. So set sail. Go love. Taste gleefully; breathe deeply. Touch. Feel.

Look around the wide, wild world as best as you can. Be untethered alone. Or tether to someone else. Or many others. Find the winding road and sell your feet to it. Make new doorways, and step through them. Find new windows, and open them. Meet new people, and see through them.

Do not be surprised to see your one and precious life. Do not be surprised to see that it is in colour.

FOREWORD

B.A. Van Sise is an author and photographic artist focused on the intersection between language and the visual image. He is the author of two monographs: the visual poetry anthology *Children of Grass: A Portrait of American Poetry* with Mary-Louise Parker, and *Invited to Life: After the Holocaust* with Neil Gaiman, Mayim Bialik, and Sabrina Orah Mark. He has previously been featured in solo exhibitions at the Center for Creative Photography, the Center for Jewish History and the Museum of Jewish Heritage, as well as in group exhibitions at the Peabody Essex Museum, the Museum of Photographic Arts, the Los Angeles Center of Photography and the Whitney Museum of American Art; a number of his portraits of American poets are in the permanent collection of the Smithsonian's National Portrait Gallery. His short nonfiction and poetry has been featured in *Poets & Writers, The North American Review, Nowhere, the Los Angeles Review, Tupelo Quarterly, The Southampton Review, Eclectica, Cutleaf,* and *The Intrepid Times*, and he is a frequent reviewer of poetry and photography titles for the *New York Journal of Books*. He has been a finalist for the Rattle Poetry Prize, the Travel Media Awards for feature writing, and the Meitar Award for Excellence in Photography. He is a 2022 New York State Council on the Arts Fellow in Photography, a Prix de la Photographie Paris award-winner, and an Independent Book Publishers Awards gold medallist.

Introduction

~~~

Around 2015, I sat in a cafe in a small European city and watched a seminar on the theme of 'How to be a digital nomad'. The cafe was packed with people around university age, clutching beers or lattes, and wearing expressions of earnestness.

I'd been a digital nomad myself in China, and now Eastern Europe, for the better part of two years and was at the event with a mixed group of local and international friends. Some were students; others were freelancers and nomadic types like me. We were there out of curiosity as this kind of event was unusual in this part of the world at that time, but most of the audience showed up looking eager and earnest.

The audience was there to learn. Their goals were to see the world, work as they travelled, and engineer lives of freedom. They had questions about how to go about doing this. And the speaker had promised answers.

The speaker was a young man of around 30, who had close-cropped black hair that was balding at the temples, and was wearing a rumpled, unbuttoned shirt worn loosely over a T-shirt, orange chinos and Converse shoes.

He took the mic, introduced himself, and showed a series of slides. There he was, shirtless, working on his laptop by a beach in Thailand. There he was, also shirtless, by a pool in the Dominican Republic. There he was in a bar, laptop poised next to a pint glass.

'I've been fortunate to travel to 32 countries,' he said, 'and I believe that investing in travel experience is the best thing you can do with the money you earn. Who agrees with me?'

Many hands shot up, including my own.

'I am a digital nomad. I have lived and worked in Asia and in the Caribbean and in Europe, and my life is amazing!'

He spoke for about 20 minutes, showing more slides. The promise was that he would teach people how to live such a lifestyle. And he did give some advice …

'When you are on video conferences with clients, don't point your camera at the beach …'

'Always do your work before you have the first pint!'

'Work with clients who you like, and who have missions that inspire you!'

'Make your lifestyle your business.'

After a few more such phrases, he wrapped up. I lingered, speaking with the attendees. They were confused, to say the least. The advice given seemed to make an assumption: that people would already have profitable businesses that they could take with them around the world.

But most people in the audience were not successful entrepreneurs. They were students, teachers and office workers. They wanted to have this promised lifestyle, but they knew they needed to learn more about how to achieve it. And they left the event disappointed.

The truth is, a lot of digital nomad-entrepreneur types, especially a few years ago, simply got lucky. They had an in-demand skill, such as programming or copywriting, and worked in open-minded industries like tech which accepted workers with unconventional lifestyles. Their skillsets happened to align with the market, and the result was freedom.

But what if you're not a coder? What if you don't work in tech? How then do you program yourself into this amazing, promised digital-nomad lifestyle?

Answers can be hard to find, and so-called 'gurus' can be so into selling the lifestyle, they often overlook the basics. *Untethered* sets out to correct this.

In this book you will receive a direct, unvarnished account of what being a digital nomad is actually like, written by someone who has been living the life for close to seven years. You will meet various other 'digital nomads' who have found their own paths to location independent living. You will learn how entrepreneurs (who did not simply get lucky) deliberately created lifestyle businesses that they could operate remotely, and you'll learn the steps to take and the skills required to emulate them, if you choose to do so.

You will also meet remote workers, many of whom were empowered by recent shifts in the workplace driven by the global pandemic, who have found themselves liberated from the office and free to work from wherever they choose. You'll encounter creatives who are not passionate about money but have found a way to make a living from their chosen craft or art form, at least enough to keep the lights on and the suitcase packed.

Looking at the opportunities and disruptions caused by the pandemic, but also resisting seeing everything through the lens of this event, it is my goal here to give you an honest take on what the so-called 'digital nomad revolution' has actually led to. We'll talk about both the good (the chance meetings in bars that lead to future clients, the exotic countries, exhilarating freedom and adventure) and the bad (the administration, the anxiety of trying to figure out the logistics of an unconventional life, the constant need to be 'plugged in') and the realization that if you manage to work from anywhere, then you may just end up working from everywhere.

By the end of *Untethered*, you will know whether or not the digital nomad life — or some slice of it — is right for you. And if you decide that it is, you will understand how to go about it based on your unique skills, goals, preferences and motivations. I do believe that we are living in a unique moment where access to the world is more available than most people realize, and that when we separate our concepts of identity from the place where we were born, we can become more interesting, open-minded and thoughtful people.

It is my hope that you will be able to learn from, and avoid, some of the many mistakes I have made, that some of the misadventures will at least make for entertaining reading, and the examples from my own life and others will help you become aware of possibilities that you may not otherwise have considered.

The legendary travel writer Paul Theroux wrote that he had never heard a train go by without wishing he was on it. Paul was an

American who lived much of his life in England, both great railway nations. I grew up in New Zealand, a remote island in the South Pacific with a sparse railway network. The only real means of escape was to fly, and so airplanes (*ear-plynes* in the local accent) stuck in my mind.

As a child, the economy-class seat seemed enormous on the long-haul flight from Auckland to Singapore. The television screen located in the back of the seat in front of me kept me riveted (I remember watching *The Jungle Book* and a game called Kirby), while the hostesses would spoil me with free snacks. Singapore airport was a fascinating wonderland, with rooms of holograms and games. We would then continue on to London to see the parents who my parents had left behind when they emigrated shortly before my birth. The connection in Singapore was sometimes long enough to allow for a brief excursion into the city state. I don't recall if it was with my mother or father (I did this journey frequently with each of them, but never in memory with them both) with whom I rode that very first taxi into Asia, but I can still remember the towering building resplendent with mystical Chinese characters and garish neon signs, a billion hawkers and sharp smells and strange noises. Everything was different and magical. I stood up to my full four- or five-year-old height on the back seat of the taxi and took it all in.

Through primary school my dad would bring back small model airplanes from his many trips and I would worship them from my suburban Auckland bedroom. In high school I knew, intuitively, I would take the so-called 'gap year' and delay university to see a bit of the world. I'd been working part-time and had saved up enough to buy a pass for 20,000 kilometres on Australia's Greyhound bus network. I planned to hop from bus to youth hostel until the money ran out or I figured out something better to do. The journey began in Sydney and took me to every state and territory in Australia. Small roadhouses outside beat-up desert mining towns replaced the spotless splendour of Singapore airport, the crash of a kangaroo against the bull bars on the roaring bus substituted for the airplane TV and enticing snack trolley. I was off and, other than for a few mostly sedentary years at university in isolated Dunedin that drove the wanderlust to a frenzy, I've never really stopped.

Travel, to me and so many others whom I hope have reached for this book, is not a break from life but a way of life. It is that feeling of belonging both everywhere and nowhere. It is feeling restless after a few months (or weeks) at home. It is the terror of thinking you know what tomorrow will bring. What next Monday will bring. And the Monday after that.

But this vagabondish existence seems to run counter to the normal goals and milestones of adulthood. If you're constantly on the move, you aren't forging stable, sustaining relationships. You aren't nurturing a career. You aren't building a credit rating or paying down a mortgage. You are moving, but perhaps you aren't growing. This may be fine for a year or so in order to find yourself, but forever ... for life ... surely you'll just be left behind?

The costs are real. I remember when I visited two successful lawyer friends in Hong Kong, and because I'd splurged on the trip, I had to suggest, a little weakly, that perhaps we go to a cheaper restaurant to eat. They too had travelled and even relocated to exotic lands as expats. But they'd also achieved some of the conventional milestones. I am not sure if this was a wake-up call of sorts, or whether it was the terror of the pandemic when a reliable income sourced cratered and I had to hustle to save an income, or entering my fourth decade and requiring something softer than the hostel floor, or being in a long-term relationship and wanting the stability and comfort that brings, but at some point I started putting a bit less energy into pushing the 'freedom and adventure' lever, and a bit more on the 'work hard and build shit' lever.

Opportunities came, and I built what was essentially a make-ends-meet freelance writing business into an agency and income source that would be considered respectable (if unspectacular), even by those who were not currently living out of suitcases in the quiet corners of the Balkans and Eastern Europe.

While the uncertainty of travel has put strain on personal relationships at times (there are only so many times you can tell a glamorous woman that she can own so many clothes as to fit in one suitcase, with shoes metered out by the inch and by the gram), travelling for years at a time with my partner proved that we could survive discomfort together, overcome early starts and late nights stranded in strange lands, cope with uncertainty and overcome challenges. All useful skills. My point is, while the digital nomad life is an unconventional and counterintuitive route to the conventional milestones of happiness and success, it does not need to preclude you from them.

Some nomads whom you will meet in these pages are happy to prioritize adventure over income, solitude and freedom over calm and company. Others own homes, run businesses or have high-powered corporate careers with six-figure incomes all while travelling long term. And most, like me, are a little confused but mostly content, somewhere in between. Wherever you see yourself on that spectrum, if the passing of a plane overhead fills you with a mixture of excitement and anxious wanderlust, then you are in the right place.

An American expat journalist I met in Tbilisi told me if he goes for too many days without writing, he 'gets a little weird'. Likewise for me with travel (and writing too, for that matter). Some need to know where they will be sleeping next month, next year. Others need that calming cup of chamomile tea, the presence of a beloved pet, the satisfaction of exceeding a milestone or reaching a professional goal.

Beginnings

About eight years ago, a younger, slimmer version of me was sitting in a small, cramped bar in Poznan, a university town in the west of Poland. The bar was a typical student joint, and back then I was young enough to blend in. Typical for Poland, anyway. It was underground. It was dark. The music was loud but not too loud for conversation. Top 40 stuff and the odd Polish rock classic that will get everyone singing along. Beers went for about AU$1 each. Young people sprawled around tables, while the older, more weathered crowd sat upstairs at a bar.

Fetching a round of drinks for myself and a friend, I stood behind an old man who had just ordered four shots of vodka, filled to the brim, and a large glass of orange juice. Like a mechanic adding fluids to a car engine or a doctor administering pills, the old man took the first shot. His face expressionless, he followed it with a sip of the orange juice. The next shot went down just as smoothly, followed by more juice. The third and the fourth quickly disappeared, and within the space of 30 seconds all five glasses stood empty.

'Co chcesz?' ('What do you want?')

The bartender, utterly unfazed by the performance of the old man, snapped me out of my awestruck reverie. I grabbed two beers and took them back to the table where my friend was waiting.

We were the only ones in the bar speaking English, and back then, in certain less-visited spots, this would still warrant the occasional curious glance. Some well-dressed guys in their late twenties were working on laptops at a table behind us, beers scattered among the keyboards and cables. The eldest, who was tall, slim with a wispy goatee, pale skin and short, spiky black hair, looked at me as I finished telling a story to my friend. He walked over. 'Where are you from?'

'New Zealand.'

'New Zealand, wow! What are you doing here?'

'Just staying for a few months, checking it out.'

'Amazing, hey … can you help me with an article I'm writing in English?'

By then I was pretty accustomed to odd encounters with strangers in Europe, but this was new. Sure, this kind of thing happened a lot when I lived in China, where friends of friends of friends tracked down my contact details and asked me to rewrite a 50,000 word thesis as a favour, but it had never happened here.

'Okay,' I said. What the heck.

I sat at his laptop and looked at the document. It was a typical piece of 'content', an article designed to attract clicks and maybe customers, focused on a fairly specific part of web development and design. I started editing, correcting grammar errors and smoothing over the verbiage. I lost myself in the task, much to the annoyance of the young lady I was with, and handed back the article to the man with a flourish.

'This is amazing,' he said, reading through. 'Hey,' he looked at me intently. 'Do you want a job?'

I wasn't working at the time. I'd put myself through university with an online business selling ebooks and courses. Selling the business had given me enough cash to disappear into China for six months and then find myself in Europe. I hadn't yet developed the writing habit and didn't have much to fill the days other than reading and wandering the old city. 'Why not?' I thought.

So began a several-month spell of early morning trams to an office in an up-and-coming suburb, where I'd write and edit articles about web development with a small team of Poles led by a maniacal Turkish man with an impressive beard and a picture of Mustafa Kemal Atatürk (the founding father of the Republic of Turkey) as his screensaver. The work was dull and the pay humiliating, but it was, in some ways, my gateway into the world of professional copywriting and content marketing.

Other clients would come from similarly random encounters. A major client whom I've worked with now for half a decade was also met in a bar. Another was an introduction from a friend. My biggest current client at the time of writing found me on LinkedIn when I updated my location status a few months after moving to Spain.

During this particular chapter in Poznan, I attended the 'digital nomad' seminar I mentioned earlier, where the well-coiffed young man spoke about how amazing his life was and how anyone could quit their job and work from Thailand. He was pretty light on the 'how'. As my career has advanced, I've found myself writing less and less 'copy' and doing more of the big picture stuff, directing tone and messaging for organizations, developing marketing strategy, figuring out how products are going to be sold and to whom. However, writing is still a big part of my work, and chipping away at the craft is satisfying and interesting, while at times frustrating and even terrifying. In the corporate space, feedback is rigid, immediate and brutal. Your writing is 'good' if people buy what you are selling. It is 'bad' if they do not. There is no escape from this calculation. When you've had entire corporations poring over your precious words, tearing them apart, and leaving your beautiful copy whimpering feebly in the recycling bin, then you're unlikely to be discouraged by a form rejection letter from a literary magazine or a one-star review on Amazon.

The 2020 pandemic reality has ironically helped with this lifestyle in some ways. Companies that previously wanted people 'in the room' have adapted to welcome more remote workers, which has resulted in more work for me. People are also generally a little more tolerant of those who reject the corporate lifestyle in favour of something a little more autonomous. And those of us used to the uncertain world of freelancing have, in some ways, more practice at the constant adaptation that this new world requires from us. It hasn't always been easy. While many people fall into a life that is designed for them, consciously or otherwise, you're going to have to deliberately design yourself from the ground up. Here, we'll look at the 'how'.

1

Meet the
digital nomad

~~~

There was a time when you couldn't turn your head without seeing someone promoting the 'digital nomad' lifestyle. Runaway bestsellers like Tim Ferris's *4-Hour Workweek* promoted freedom and the life of your dreams being just a few keyboard strokes away. The 9 to 5 was for suckers. Learn a few simple secrets and limitless travel awaits.

Maybe you were tempted. Maybe you still have a copy of that book on your shelf, or ads popping up on your Facebook timeline. Maybe you flirted with the idea of being a nomad … but life has a way of, well, getting in the way. Borders closed and then opened again. Life got more expensive. Work got busy. Time passed. Books gathered dust on the shelf. And the dream faded … Or maybe you took the other path, the road less travelled by. You set out, passport and laptop in hand, to conquer the world one Wi-Fi hotspot at a time. *Untethered* is for those who have made — or are tempted to make — this second choice, and what it actually looks like. You'll be able to peak behind the curtain at the real face of the digital nomad lifestyle. You will discover that, far from the ripped Instagram models sipping piña coladas by MacBooks in Thailand, the real face of long-term travel can look a bit more like this:

» Thom Brown: An English travel writer who, despite starting from almost zero barely a year ago, now lives and travels the world on the back of his writing, and he'll explain exactly how he does it.

» Nora Dunn: A Canadian business owner, blogger and speaker, one of the 'OG' digital nomads, she is a leading expert on how digital nomads finance their lives and travels. She shares her personal story and experience.

» Jennifer Roberts: The editor and customer service manager who performs a range of communication, writing and project management jobs remotely from bases as far afield as South America and Eastern Europe, between occasional visits home to Illinois.

» Barry Kirkham: A British businessman and graphic designer who networked and hustled his way to turning a small local magazine into a global business that he runs from the branches of Brazil and the cafes of Poland.

» Enrique Hygge: The Florida-born business owner who used the connections he made while living in Asia to launch his own widget company with just a few hundred dollars to his name. The risk paid off and his seven-figure business now takes him around the world on his own terms.

» Sarah Cash: An American globetrotter who works remotely for a travel company and has been exploring the world virtually non-stop since she was fresh out of high school.

» Raven Patzke: The former Los Angeles barista who quit her job and reinvented herself as the globetrotting virtual assistant to a famous artist.

» Cathy Raymond: An English teacher from the United States who has lived and travelled in some of the most challenging and exotic countries on the fringes of Europe and Asia, like Afghanistan, Tajikistan and Uzbekistan.

» Ivy Raff: The former remote software implementation manager who travelled the world solving complex coding problems and now enjoys a more relaxed (but equally global) life as a multi-talented freelancer for a range of diverse clients.

» Harry Cunningham: A Kiwi (New Zealand) expat in London who manages to take his project management job on the road for months at a time, working out of Greece or Poland or Italy as part of his company's remote-work plan.

» Bart Och: The Anglo-Polish photographer, entrepreneur and editor who manages to eke out enough income strictly from his passions to travel the world on a budget, going wherever his soul leads him.

» Henry Worsley: The swashbuckling young journalist and drop-in tour guide, who dashes off to the likes of Kyrgyzstan or Ukraine while taking breaks from his English literature degree at Oxford University.

» Justin Dynia: An American political communication specialist with a full-time job for a congressman who spends months of the year working with a laptop from the cafes of Spain, France and Portugal.

Some of the examples above will resonate with you, and some won't. As we go through, you'll discover a menu of options that you can mix and match as you create a location-independent lifestyle that works for you. You'll be prepared for some of the bumps you're likely to encounter on the road, and will have learned some potent skills you can apply to other aspects of your work and home life, even if you decide (like many people do) that staying home is best for you, after all.

Throughout this book, you'll hear from all of the digital nomads mentioned above in their own words. They'll talk honestly about their experiences, where they have lived and travelled, their advice for you, and what they wish they knew when they were first starting out. Some have written extensively and emotionally; others are more clipped and casual. My intention has been to preserve their authentic voices with as little editing as possible to showcase the true diversity of the kinds of people who can become digital nomads. Not everyone is a swashbuckling wanderer. Not everyone is a financial genius travel hacker. Here, we'll meet them all so you can understand the differences. You will resonate with and agree with some of what you read, and others won't quite fit with you. That's the point: digital nomads are all different. You will see things you can select, embrace and learn from in order to become the kind of long-term traveller who you (may) want to be.

MEET THE NOMADS

Name: Nora Dunn

Canadian, in her mid-forties.

Mostly travels: Sometimes alone, sometimes with friends or her partner.

Currently in: Toronto, Canada.

Digital nomad experience: Twelve years.

Has lived/worked/travelled in: The USA, Australia, New Zealand, Indonesia, Thailand, Vietnam, Bulgaria, Switzerland, France, Spain, UK, Ireland, Sweden, Grenada, Panama, Costa Rica, Ecuador, Peru, Colombia, Mexico, St Martin and Greece.

Normally stays in a country/city for: Two or three months.

Makes a living as a: Entrepreneur, founder of The Professional Hobo (https://www.theprofessionalhobo.com).

Meet Nora

The current centrepiece of my online career is The Professional Hobo (https://www.theprofessionalhobo.com), a website I've run since I became a digital nomad in 2006. I'm recognized as one of the 'OG' digital nomads and travel bloggers. On my site I not only share my adventures and misadventures alike, but I also help people design their lifestyles and arrange their affairs so they can travel long-term while working remotely. I coined the term 'Financially Sustainable Travel' as part of this process. You can find all my social channels and other outlets on the website. I am also a freelance writer. I write about travel, personal finance, and lifestyle design. As a former Certified Financial Planner, I parlay my financial expertise with my travel experience to dominate the niche of the finance of travel. I am currently a writer and spokesperson for NerdWallet.

How Nora got started

In 2006 I sold everything I owned in Canada (including a busy financial planning practice) to embrace my dreams of travelling the world long-term, in a culturally immersive way. Concepts like 'digital nomad', 'location independent', and even 'remote work' hadn't yet been envisaged, so there was no infrastructure for people like me.

Along the way I carved out a remote career as a freelance writer, and as blogging turned from glorified online journals into a bona fide industry, I became known as one of 'the first' travel bloggers and digital nomads.

I have been a digital nomad since 2006, though after twelve years of full-time travel, I now have a home base in Toronto that I spend at least a couple of months of the year at.

Nora's 'typical day'

When the world around me is always changing, it's important to have some continuity in my routine so that I remain grounded and productive. Thus, I have a pretty solid morning routine that includes exercise and meditation. I also tend to get to work right away and then enjoy whatever destination I'm at in the afternoon and evening, but I'm flexible to whatever the circumstances present.

Nora's favourite thing about the 'digital nomad' life is ...

When I close my laptop for the day, I have a new backyard to discover. Even as a new place becomes familiar and I learn how to live and function there, I always feel like a traveller.

Her least favourite thing about the 'digital nomad' life is ...

I suffered a profound episode of burnout after twelve years on the road because I had lost all sense of belonging. This was because I never made an effort to connect and collaborate with other digital nomads, and this lack of community proved my downfall. I think there's a balance to be struck between living in a culturally immersive way and socializing with other people who share the same lifestyle/career structure/priorities.

The number one thing Nora wished she knew when she first started out as a digital nomad is ...

The travel lifestyle is work! It's like a job unto itself and takes a monumental amount of time and energy. It's important to allow for this and set a pace of travel that is sustainable and rewarding.

2

Myth-busting the digital nomad

~~

So much has been said about the digital nomad lifestyle that the reality is often masked under layers of hype. Many of the most visible self-proclaimed digital nomads have created a biased or unrealistic picture of what most digital nomads are really like, so it may help to begin with a quick primer on what digital nomads are not, before getting into what digital nomads are.

Digital nomads are not (all) ...

To many readers, the term 'digital nomad' will bring certain images and stereotypes to mind. Many of these have been created by advertisers trying to sell a lifestyle, and are oversimplified media depictions. The truth is far more nuanced and diverse ... as the following list below outlines.

» Social media influencers. Many digital nomads even manage to get through entire days or even weeks without posing on Instagram or uttering the word 'selfie'.

» Young techies. Some are, of course, but I am meeting more and more nomads at later stages of life, and my completely unscientifically based guess of the average age of the digital nomad would be somewhere in the mid-thirties.

» Entrepreneurs. Hustle culture is alive and well in the digital nomad community, but many also have much more stable and conventional income streams, such as working an 'ordinary' (remote) job.

» Constantly on the move. While it can be fun to switch countries every three days, it's not great for getting things done. Spending months, even as long as a year, in one place is an increasingly common approach.

» Childless. Although most digital nomads I have met are not yet parents, you will encounter some who travel with young children under school age. While this presents its own unique challenges that this book will not attempt to explore and I am not expert in, the business, work and life tips will still very much apply to those in this situation.

» Rich. Incomes for digital nomads vary widely from a few hundred dollars per month to tens of thousands, and in this book we'll meet people from across the spectrum.

» American or Australian. While coming from a relatively wealthy country with a powerful passport is a huge advantage, digital nomads from Eastern Europe and Asia are becoming more and more common.

» Life-long nomads. Some live the long-term travel life for just a few months; others for years. And some indeed never stop.

Successful digital nomads are …

In a nutshell, digital nomads are people who work online while travelling abroad. They may be Americans living in Europe, or Europeans living in South-East Asia. They may be entrepreneurs or virtual assistants, young or old, single or in a couple (or even a family). They are typically curious and highly motivated by new experiences. It also helps if they are …

» Organized. Digital nomad lives can get complicated, especially when you are juggling finances across multiple currencies, dealing with complex visa rules, living life in unfamiliar cultures and languages, and all while working a full-time job or running a business!

» Adaptable and resilient. All long-term travellers know that things go wrong on the road! From closed borders to lost luggage, unexpected power cuts and dodgy Wi-Fi, digital nomads need to be resourceful and able to quickly adapt to changing circumstances.

» (Exceptionally) passionate about travel. If the thrill of arriving in a new place does not overpower the fear and frustration that come with the challenges of living and working far from home, then you will probably soon be booking a return ticket (and that's fine too!).

» (A little) nuts. To eschew the security, comfort and predictability of a 'normal' life and knowingly opt into an extra dose of hassle and complexity, all for the thrill of it or simply because you know you cannot do otherwise, probably means you're a little bit atypical.

Far from a distraction from the real world, being a digital nomad can provide great training that will help you excel even when you're staying still. Especially in a world as unstable as ours keeps insisting on being.

The uncertainty advantage

It takes a long time to write a book. And our world changes fast. At the start of my writing process, the COVID-19 pandemic was battering the world for the fourth (or was it fifth?) time. And now, as I come to the final stages, the pandemic seems to have faded away. Neither gone nor forgotten, but not in front of mind every second of every day, as it has been much of the past two years.

However, things change, and by the time this book reaches your doorstep, we may again be living a dystopian existential battle. Or we may truly have moved on. Or … something else. It's hard not to shake a sense that the quiet, stable world we knew has gone. Maybe temporarily, maybe for good. Our world is drenched in uncertainty, and in an uncertain world perhaps travellers and nomads will be best placed to thrive.

In his book *Nomads: The wanderers who shape our world*, Anthony Sattin lays out a compelling case for how the great pivots in history and culture were caused by nomads. So-called 'settled' people built the monuments and castles, but nomads provided the spark that impelled them to do so. They brought news of a broader world, tempted people to venture beyond their doors, sparked fear and curiosity, and kept the wheels of progress turning.

While 'settled' workers will have some advantages in terms of lack of distractions, reliability of infrastructure and more immediate access to colleagues, being a nomad is its own kind of advantage. You show up when and where you choose to, on your own terms. Your assumptions are constantly challenged, forcing you to think creatively. You meet people from all over the world, learn other ways of thinking, other ways of doing things. And through the practice of travel, you become accustomed to uncertainty, accustomed to finding a way no matter what.

When we travel, we expect and even anticipate weirdness. We are prepared for things not to work. For the hotel room sheets to be stained, the border guards to be obstinate and rude, the local rules opaque and contradictory. We find it normal that people should have radically different viewpoints than ours. We embrace this chaos as a temporary break from everyday reality, something that we can check in and out of voluntarily.

With our world changing around us, we may all be travellers now, whether we choose to be or not. Over the last few years, we have all been uprooted in some way. So let's embrace, as much as we can, the opportunities inherent in this strangeness. Not being able to go home or leave home, or visit the 'obvious' places, forces us to be creative. To find stability in unfamiliar places. To live the creative life, even if we did not choose to do so, because responding to constant changes requires the breaking of habits, the challenging of old beliefs, and the creation of new ones. Being untethered is a pain, but it can also be an opportunity if we learn how to treat it as such. So now we've covered the 'what' and the 'why,' it's time to get to the 'how'!

MEET THE NOMADS

Name: Thom Brown

Mid-twenties from the United Kingdom.

Mostly travels: With his long-term partner.

Currently in: Tallinn, Estonia.

Digital nomad experience: Four or more years.

Has lived/worked/travelled in: UK, USA, Poland, Estonia, Croatia and Ghana.

Normally stays in a country/city for: A month or so.

Makes a living as a: Remote worker.

Meet Thom

Until recently, I've been a freelance travel writer. Examples of my work are on my website (https://thombrown.co.uk/) and on Instagram (@thombrowntravel). I've just been hired for a full-time travel writing role, so it's not freelance anymore but it is still remote. I now work for Projects Abroad (https://www.projects-abroad.co.uk) and will need to visit many of the destinations they offer to customers.

How Thom got started

I began with a freelance writing diploma and just started finding writing jobs online. As soon as I had something of a regular income, I went to Poland and lived in hostels for a month, writing each day to feed and house myself. Since then, I've just chosen different countries to live in while I continue to write articles online.

Thom's 'typical day'

In my new full-time role, it's a lot more structured. I wake up at 8 a.m. to start work at around 8.30. I then need to put in around eight hours, but remote work means I can be pretty flexible, as long as I'm getting the work done. I'll use my lunch break to go for walks in the local area. I'm yet to travel with this job, so it'll be interesting to see how that works out. As a freelancer, I would usually finish my day by 3 p.m. so I could spend the rest of the day exploring. Anything interesting I find would then feed into my writing work. With this new job, I'll be going to projects in places like Botswana and Nepal, so it'll be completely different from what I'm used to. Much of my job will be to simply live as a traveller and find stories for the blog. I'll interact with locals and volunteers and get to know them before coming home to write content. In the evenings, I'll have the chance to go on tours and excursions to further learn about the local culture.

Thom's favourite thing about the 'digital nomad' life is ...

(Almost) complete freedom. It can be a curse as much as a blessing, but it gives me control of how to structure my day and how to spend the vast majority of the small amount of time I have on this Earth. My favourite thing about travel is having new experiences and the growth that comes with that. My favourite thing about being a digital nomad is having the freedom to travel.

His least favourite thing about the 'digital nomad' life is ...

The lack of stability and connection to a single place. When everywhere is your home, it can sometimes feel like nowhere is your home. I don't have my own place near my hometown so going home always feels like being a guest or a temporary visitor. I have great connections in the digital nomad community, but not so many in a real physical community, which is what non-nomadic people are able to have.

The number one thing Thom wished he knew when he first started out as a digital nomad is ...

Honestly, I've loved just figuring it out on my own. I had no idea it was possible and it's been so much fun finding out that it is. I guess the one thing I would tell myself is that remote work really is the future so don't give up. Sure, it took a pandemic for many companies to realize this, but that just made it happen more quickly. (It's ironic that something that made travel impossible ended up increasing remote work opportunities, thus making it easier for many people to travel in the future.)

~~~~~~

3

Craft:

Honing a skill will get you paid from anywhere

~~~

Here's one fundamental thing the speaker at the 'digital nomad' conference I went to many years ago (see Introduction) did not explain: in order to make money, on the road or elsewhere, you generally need to be able to do something that others can't or won't do. There are exceptions and alternatives — and we'll explore some within these pages — but for the most part, digital nomads provide a service online. That is, they do something on their computer that helps people.

It's a basic law of economics that the rarer or more specialized your skill (i.e. the fewer people who can do what you do), and the more people who want your skill, the more you can charge. This is why English teachers can command high sums overseas where their native language has suddenly become a relatively rare and sought-after commodity, whereas at home it was probably not something they even thought about.

The number one way that digital nomads exchange their skills for money is as freelancers. That is, they serve a number of clients (more on these later) with their specific, developed skills. Other popular nomad pathways include entrepreneurship and remote work, both of which get their own chapters further on.

Starting with freelancers, let us establish a few handy principles that will be of use to you no matter which path you end up taking. Freelancers, in the digital nomad world at least, tend to come in fives.

The five broad types of digital freelancer

Most freelance digital nomads I've encountered fall into one of five categories, which we will explore in depth just below. Most people will immediately know which of these categories best suits their interests or talents, and all are broad enough to provide plenty of opportunity for specialization (i.e. for you to bring your unique skills to bear on the broader subject matter). The rest of this chapter will be most relevant for people who have not yet begun their digital nomad journey and/or may not yet have a career or income source. Or, if you do have one already, it's not something you want to take with you on the road (however, more and more fields now have potential for remote earning, from teaching to medicine, see below.)

If you already know what your commercial skillset is but you're unsure of how to go about getting clients who don't care what time zone you live in or what misadventures you got up to the night before with the rambunctious group of Georgian fishermen and their homebrew *chacha*, then skip to Chapter 4: Clients. If you're horrified by the idea of ever going to work for another human being as either an employee or as a freelancer, then skip right the way to Chapter 8: Entrepreneurs.

The five most common ways freelancers make money on the road

Let's look at the five broad categories of work which are in high demand and provide opportunities both for freelance work and remote employment. These are all ways that you can offer value — and I mean economic value that is sought-after — completely independent of location.

I have selected these five based on extensive interviews with many digital nomads, and also in consideration that people have different skills and attributes. We aren't all artists or designers or creatives or writers. Some of us are better at wrangling schedules or coding software. None of these requires particular qualifications — all can, to some extent, be self-taught — but they are all skilled roles that require some experience and training, and yes even a little bit of talent to pull them off. As I have written elsewhere, being a digital nomad can put your worklife on hard mode. You are going to need to be able to overdeliver value in a specific way. And it's unlikely that you're some kind of super-generalist genius who can do exceptionally well at everything. If you're like most of us mere mortals, you're going to have to specialize at least a little bit. These five categories will help you choose where to get started and establish yourself. Chances are, you already will have a sense of where you are best placed due to your work history or academic/ school life so far.

Communicators

This is my space: the copywriter or the graphic designer. People attracted to this line of work tend to have a talent or passion for writing, designing, editing or speaking, but they may not know how to monetize these talents. Often, they think it isn't possible to do so. After all, because these are skills many people are passionate about, there are many people willing to do them. To stand out, you need an edge. The best way to develop an edge as a communicator is to specialize. As with all skills, the more specialized you can be, the easier it will be to find clients and the more you will be able to charge. This means you will likely need to enhance your core talent of writing or designing with an extra layer of commercial know-how that will form the bridge between the skill you have and what clients and hiring managers are actively looking for. In short, you need to find the best way (that you are comfortable with) to use your talents to make money for someone else, and therefore make money for yourself.

As a copywriter, I have enhanced my marketability by understanding Search Engine Optimization, the techniques and technicalities of email marketing, lead nurturing, marketing psychology, and much more. Therefore, I can bill myself out as a marketing copywriter, rather than simply a 'writer'. Being a marketing copywriter is quite different from simply being a writer, in the same way that being a generic 'designer' (i.e. a person with Photoshop skills), is quite different from being a trained website designer or, better yet, a specialist ecommerce website designer.

Programmers

Programmers have always been in high demand, and that is not looking likely to change any time soon. Many of the most well-paid digital nomads I have met, from Europe to Asia, have been programmers, typically remote workers specialized in one key language, working a few days a week in exchange for enough for a comfortable lifestyle in whatever country or time zone they choose.

Familiarize yourself with the programming languages currently in demand, and you're unlikely to ever suffer much from a lack of work. In the research I undertook to see how the market looks for remote programmers right now (the turn of 2021/2022) nearly all results I found were aimed at businesses hiring programmers. In fact, chances are, if you're a programmer, you're not reading this book. You're either in an office somewhere in Seattle making six figures, or you're on a beach somewhere in the Caribbean (also making six figures!).

Organizers

This one is not where many people's minds naturally go to, but it is an increasingly important way to help companies and make a living remotely. In fact, in many of the companies I've come across, it's one of the most important roles.

Organizers are typically adept in helping remote companies keep their teams on schedule. They will be familiar with project management tools such as Trello and Jira. Their LinkedIn bio will likely say something like Project Manager or, better yet, 'Project Manager for Remote Companies'. Immediately, you have turned the fact that you are travelling the world into an asset, not a liability. If you have some corporate experience, even better. Companies are hurting for this role and this skillset. If you can make someone's life easier, or someone's business more efficient, then you are a valuable asset. Learn the lingo of project management and read as many articles as you can on organizational efficiency to get a sense of the contemporary buzzwords, then modify your pitch (more on that later) to the right kind of clients.

Customer support or social media management

Customer support and social media management fall somewhere between the communication category and the organizer category, and both can be either awful or brilliant depending on who you work for. Large companies often outsource these roles to agencies who are increasingly tolerant of remote workers; however, the roles are not considered specialized so the pay is poor and hours are often rigid. Working for startups, on the other hand, where every customer interaction is considered precious, can put you right at the core of the organization and can be rewarding.

If you are looking in this field, search for startups and emphasize the advantage your time zone gives you. For example, if you're from Canada but live in Thailand, then think about Canadian start-ups that serve the Asian market and could benefit from a native English speaker already in the target time zone.

Teaching

While teaching English in the flesh is probably the most established and least original way for people from native English-speaking countries to make a decent enough living in exotic countries, I am increasingly encountering remote teachers on my travels. Several platforms such as VIPKID, Magic Ears, Qkids Teacher and SayABC connect Western teachers to students in places like China, pay reasonably well per hour, and have absolutely no shortage of demand. This work is exhausting and the prospects for career advancement are fairly limited, not to mention the rigid hours and often inconvenient schedules, but this can be a pretty sure way to make your first dollars while getting established on the road.

And you needn't limit yourself to English. A host of languages are in demand on platforms such as Amazing Tutor, and other specialized skills, such as coding, marketing, design and more, are also sought after.

If you have specialized knowledge in any field, there will be people out there who want to learn it. Google 'Tutor [plus whatever your subject matter is]' and find out what the competition is like. Choose platforms that seem active, and put time and care into setting up your profile. Once you have a few repeat students, you may well have an income that will be enough to propel you out of the door and into the nearest airport.

No craft, no matter how polished, will earn you a cent unless you have a client willing to pay you for it. Whether you want a host of clients that you do small amounts of work for, or one main client who is your de facto employer, the techniques of getting hired are similar.

MEET THE NOMADS

Name: Jennifer Roberts

American in her late twenties.

Mostly travels: With her long-term partner.

Currently in: Poland.

Digital nomad experience: Six years.

Has lived/worked/travelled in: Thailand (one year), Chile (five years) and the United States (months at a time).

Normally stays in a country/city for: A month or so.

Makes a living as a: Remote worker.

Meet Jen

I describe myself as a freelance writer and editor, and my work is all remote. I am the Senior Editor of *Intrepid Times* and the Director of Customer Experience for TRASKA. I also work with a children's podcast editing the weekly stories, as well as for various blogs as a copyeditor.

How Jen got started

After university, I decided to take a year and work abroad as an English teacher in Thailand. It was mostly to get experience outside of my comfort zone, but I realized that I loved travelling and learning from new cultures. After Thailand, I travelled to Chile to volunteer as a teacher, and it was there that I met my partner, Felipe. I decided to stay in Chile and spent a year searching for freelance work in order to move away from teaching, which evolved into the remote jobs that I currently hold.

Jen's 'typical day'

I usually wake up around 7.30 or 8 a.m., have breakfast and drink a cup of coffee as I check my inbox and reply to emails. As I am working for four or five different companies at any given time, my workday bounces between each. The workload of each job varies, so while I may spend an hour with one job on a Monday, I may spend three hours with it on Wednesday. However, I generally work from about 8.30 to 11.30 a.m., have lunch, do yoga, rest, and then work again from about 1 to 4 or 5 p.m. If I am actively travelling, as opposed to staying at my house in Chile, I will try to work earlier in the morning in order to be done with my workday around 2 p.m. so that my partner and I can go out and explore our new location.

Jen's favourite thing about the 'digital nomad' life is ...

The freedom to travel when and where we want. Until this past year, my partner was working as an IT specialist and teacher at a local high school in Chile, so we were more limited in when and where we could travel. This year, he is also working on moving into remote work, so we are travelling for about nine months out of twelve. Being able to choose countries that we are interested in spending time in and being there for a month or more allows us to experience a place more than if we were travelling for a week or two at a time. It helps us keep life interesting and challenge ourselves by being in new places.

Her least favourite thing about the 'digital nomad' life is ...

The lack of stability. As a freelance remote worker, my salary changes monthly, which can be challenging when you're travelling for months at a time. I also can't count on health insurance or a retirement plan unless I take the time to organize those things myself. Not to mention the uncertainty around travel plans when you aren't sure if your flight will be delayed or cancelled, etc.

The number one thing Jen wished she knew when she first started out as a digital nomad is ...

It takes time to get to a place where you can feel comfortable with what you're doing. When I first started out, I was taking low-paying, mind-numbing jobs just to get experience with remote work. It took about a year for me to find online freelance work that felt genuinely fulfilling and offered decent pay. Getting started as a digital nomad, you can't expect things to fall into place quickly. You need to take the time to find the area you really want to be working in, gain experience and make contacts, which will slowly but surely get you to where you want to be. It's a process but one that is really worth it, at least from my experience.

4

Clients:
Forge profitable relationships you can maintain on the road

~~

The story I told at the start of this book about meeting a copywriting client in a bar is an entertaining yarn and was an exciting moment I often think about. That one client, however, ended up being fairly short lived, and negligible in terms of pay. Most clients I've worked with I've acquired the old-fashioned way, using techniques that, unlike hanging out in bars waiting for people to ask you to write something, are actually replicable regardless of your circumstances or profession.

We'll look at a few of the most surefire ways to connect with clients and remote employers, but first let's look at the difference between two popular forms of remote work: the 'gig' economy, and long-term clients.

Freelancing: Gigs vs clients

The appeal of freelance is in the name (the 'free' part, unless your name happens to be Lance, in which case you're winning double). As a freelancer, your income is typically divided among a small-ish number of clients, or large-ish number of gigs. While definitions vary, here we'll look at clients as companies you serve on an ongoing basis with some kind of ongoing commitment, whereas gigs are one-off jobs you do for a set fee.

The so-called 'gig economy' gets a hard rap in the media these days, with the spotlight on delivery-app drivers who are often portrayed as open to exploitation. As a digital nomad, you can also expose yourself to some similar traps: paid rates on networks like Fiverr can be a race to the bottom, and unpaid invoices for work you have already done can be painful, both emotionally and financially. For these reasons, I strongly suggest you work on cultivating long-term relationships with reliable clients, rather than setting yourself up for an endless series of smaller gigs.

At the time of writing, I currently work with four companies, all of whom I've had some sort of business relationship with for at least three years. There are many benefits to working with people over the long term, including:

» Trust. This is a two-way street. The client trusts you to deliver work to a high standard, and you trust them to pay the agreed fee on time and without hassle.

» Improvement. Especially if you are a creative like a copywriter or designer, long-term knowledge of a client's business allows you to exponentially increase your efficiency as you learn about the market and gather feedback on what's working. This leads to better outcomes for both of you. Improving your skills is important for your long-term career/business growth, and your client will get more and more value from your work, and likely pay you more overtime as well.

» Responsibility. Companies that are growing fast may reward your loyalty with opportunities to play a larger role. This can result in you being able to command higher fees, and also be rewarding in itself as you help businesses you believe in evolve and achieve exciting things.

UNTETHERED

Understanding clients

A client is someone who pays you to do a service for them. They are distinct from a customer, who buys a thing from you, and an employer, who is typically your sole (or at least main) source of income and who owns your time on a long-term, full-time or part-time basis.

The best clients are those you work for on a long-term, recurring basis. These can be companies of any size, though smaller businesses where you can deal directly with the owner are often more flexible and willing to entertain more unconventional working styles, such as you cropping up in a different time zone every few weeks! That's not to say large businesses and corporations can't make good regular clients — ultimately, every client wants the same thing: the knowledge that the work they need to get done will actually get done in an effective and timely manner. And if you can prove that you are able to provide this, you should be able to maintain the client relationship without too much difficulty. Of course, as in all personal and business relationships, some tact is often required. A good client is:

» an owner of a business or a department manager of a larger business whom you find it easy to communicate with

» someone who sets clear expectations, provides articulate and constructive feedback, and does not change the scope of a project halfway through

» someone who respects that good work deserves to be well paid and, while not reckless with money, is more interested in quality work than hunting for a bargain

» someone who is in a business that is growing and sees your work as important to that growth. This means there's a long-term place for you, and also that your work is seen as an asset to be maximized, rather than an expense to be minimized

» someone who understands that you are a client and not an employee, and therefore will not be on call all day, every day.

There are no perfect clients. At the start of your career you may need to compromise a little bit, but as you grow in demand and stature, and get more experienced working with clients and educating them about your expectations, you will be able to structure mutually beneficial relationships that work for you on your own terms.

Managing client relationships over time is a subtle art and will depend a lot on the nature of your work, the kinds of business/ individuals you are working with, and your own career goals. For many people reading this, managing clients is a purely hypothetical concern! After all, before you can worry about managing clients you first have to get them! And that's what we're going to look at in the most detail first.

Sharpening your pitch

Earlier, we looked at how digital nomads make money by doing something that others can't or won't do. Your pitch is a statement that explains how you do that. Marketers call this a value proposition, and it's extremely important when crafting this to think not only of yourself, but also the kinds of clients you want to serve.

How to define your value proposition

Below are some questions that can help you get started in working out what your value proposition is.

» Would you rather work for startups, entrepreneurs, small businesses or large corporations?

- Startups will typically be fast-paced and a little chaotic, but there's potential for a huge upside if the company succeeds and grows.

- Entrepreneurs means managing a relationship directly with the business owner, who may also be the only employee. This works well if (and only if) you have a good, trusting relationship with them.

- Small businesses mean you may have a relationship with the head of a department, like the marketing chief, creating a layer of separation between you and the big boss. This may mean more stability, but also you may feel more disconnected from the results of your work.

- Corporations mean following rigid processes and often feeling like a small cog in a very big machine. However, your invoices will almost certainly be paid on time, and the company is unlikely to go out of business at the drop of a hat.

» Do you have a preferred industry you would like to work for?

» How many clients would you like to serve? A handful? A few dozen? Just one? (If so, you may want to skip to Chapter 7: Employers.)

» What will you do for these clients? (For example, provide copy, do graphic design, manage projects, handle customers.)

» What value will this service provide? Try and think of the business goal behind this. For example, writing copy = increasing sales. Customer support = increasing satisfaction and customer loyalty.

» What allows you to provide this skill at a high level? If you have experience, great! If not, think about the attributes you have that would apply, for example: detail oriented, meticulous, data-driven. Think about ways you can prove this in your pitch.

When you have an idea of who you are serving and what value you provide, then work on putting this together in a snappy paragraph. Remember, the more specific you can be, the better. Some examples are below.

» Results-driven copywriter specialized in high-converting email copy for the education industry.

» Creative graphic designer specialized in deploying web-friendly assets for the non-profit sector.

» Detail-oriented project manager specialized in helping startups transition to a remote-first approach.

Now you've done the most important work, it's time to flaunt it! Here are three approaches for approaching potential clients and putting your newly acquired positioning skills to work.

1. **LinkedIn:** I've been offered several opportunities via LinkedIn, which has been responsible for one of my most lucrative and rewarding clients. Set up your LinkedIn profile with as much detail as possible, and use the positioning above to flesh out your description. If you don't have any experience, create some! Write an article about your project management philosophy, and/or share some example

graphics. Be active. Participate helpfully in discussions, and start paying attention to the kind of companies who may fit your client criteria and are looking to hire someone like you. Use the LinkedIn search bar and key search terms, such as 'Fashion startups Boston' or whichever terms best fit your criteria. Follow them and interact with their posts, and also follow some of their employees. Mention them (helpfully) in a few posts of your own, get to know the key people, and then offer your services to the most relevant personnel.

2. **Your current network:** Clients may not have magically materialized from your network previously, simply because people may not previously have known what you do. The more specialized your positioning, the more likely this is to happen. I've had referrals from people I've never ever met, whom I've merely interacted with online, as I am the person who comes to mind for them when they think 'copywriter'. Ask yourself how you can make this clear in the minds of others you associate with as well. Building a dynamic and interesting LinkedIn profile is a good start!

3. **Expat forums and meetups:** If you're already overseas, or even if you only have destinations in mind, check out expat forums on Facebook. Search for digital nomad meetup groups and couchsurfing meetups and, as we explored above, participate helpfully in the conversations. I've ended up with clients through this approach, largely because I went into these situations, online and in person, with the goal of providing value and making friends. First, establish real connections, then people will be genuinely motivated to find out

what you do. And if you do this enough and have your positioning sorted, opportunities will come up. Over seven years of 'nomading' all over the world, opportunities have kept happening for me, and they will for you as well.

In a nutshell, the key to getting clients is to know what value you provide and to who, and to mix with people who might be able to give you opportunities. It can take time, but it's not rocket science. The better you understand and hone your value proposition, and the more you figure out helpful ways to flaunt it, the more opportunities will start chasing you. In time, you'll be turning jobs away!

Working with clients: Expectations and value

Now that you have an opportunity to work with a client, you probably have a couple of important questions, such as, 'How much do you charge?' and 'How do you make sure they are happy with your work and will want to hire you again or make a referral?' Both issues are related, so we'll tackle them one by one.

First, the pricing issue. Depending on the field you are in, you are likely to receive a lot of contradictory advice on this. Some say you should never ever have an hourly rate as a freelancer. Some say you must. I've tried every pricing model under the sun, from charging per word to per hour to monthly retainers to a percentage of sales, and right now I still use a mix of all of the above! A good client relationship will be a custom one where you and the client develop a solution that suits you both. I would advise against being dogmatic here: figure out models that you are comfortable with, iterate and change when you feel like you're being underpaid or if clients stop coming back because you're perceived as too expensive.

On the question of the amount to charge, philosophies also abound here and, in my opinion, a lot of in-vogue advice will lead to freelancers pricing themselves out of the market. Yes, freelancers do need to charge more on average per hour than full-time employees because the work is less steady. But clients don't really care about the bills you have to pay. They care about their business. Therefore, the best way to succeed with pricing and command steadily higher rates is to become an expert in communicating the value of your service to your clients.

Gather data to help you make an argument for how your work earns or saves your client money. Talk about increased conversion rates, or increased efficiency, or reduced costs. Connect your work to their business goals, and stress the benefits your clients will get from hiring you. Do this right, and clients won't see you as an annoying expense, but as an asset to be invested in to the full. As a client recently said to me when I asked for extra pay on a project because its scope had expanded: 'We need as much of your time as you can spare.'

In three short steps, to make yourself as attractive to potential clients as possible:

1. Determine what value you provide.

2. Announce this to the world.

3. Track and prove this to your clients.

It can take a while, especially if you're starting from scratch, to develop a successful freelance business. You'll make mistakes, have to ditch some clients and be ditched by others, and probably rethink your value proposition many times as you evolve. You may need to, as I have, take some gigs along the way which are less well paid and much less exciting than you would like. This helps sharpen the saw and improve your skills not only at the job you're doing, but also at the more subtle art of managing clients. The sooner you start, the sooner you will be in a position where you're happy to unplug your laptop, head to the airport, and run your business from the skies.

Coping when things go wrong

'I am not going to be able to pay this invoice,' the client wrote. One month of work, at long-established rates, and this had not been mentioned. These things happen to freelancers but they do not happen to employees. And whereas once the benefit of being able to work from anywhere was a novelty, a gift, in the world of remote work and pandemic lockdowns, it had suddenly become neither as unique nor as desirable as before.

So, client, how am I to pay the bills, buy food and carry on with the costly business of life, after having spent a month writing for you, for apparently no pay?

It was late 2020, and our final weeks in Poland, staying in the quiet city of Kalisz where my girlfriend's family had an apartment that was empty and available for us rent free. The apartment was warm and wooden and on the second floor of a crumbling stone building about ten minutes' walk from the sleepy town centre. Entering through the corridor, you inhaled the strong scent of cabbage and encountered one of two old ladies who lived along the way. One was fat and jolly and conspired with us; the other thin and bitter and malevolent. You almost never passed by unnoticed by either.

In the winter older Poles burn whatever they can find in their furnaces and the air becomes metallic and tainted, not on the level of China's smog, but enough to make fresh air elusive and breathing unpleasant. The restaurants of the town closed and our escape was to take the bus to the nearby lake, where we drank beer, played music and wandered among the forest.

There was little else to do but work. And so when the client in question blithely denied payment for the services I'd offered, I fortunately had others to turn to. Getting more work from existing clients is easier than acquiring new ones. I sent an email to a Spanish American company I'd been doing copywriting work for, and they agreed to double the size of our project that we were working on together. That would tide us over.

Often, your existing clients are your greatest potential source of extra work when times are tough. Colleagues in sales call this 'land and expand'. These clients trust you, and you have spent time learning their business. When one fails, you don't always need to start from scratch if you have enough of a network of existing clients on the go. Of course, first you're going to need to become very good at attracting clients. And for that, I'm afraid to say, you're gonna need a brand ... That's what we will look at in the next chapter.

MEET THE NOMADS

Name: Raven Patzke

American in her mid-twenties.

Mostly travels: Alone, and recently with her long-term partner.

Currently in: Los Angeles, California.

Digital nomad experience: About two years.

Has lived/worked/travelled in: The USA, Australia, Iceland, El Salvador, Mexico, France, Portugal, the Bahamas, Thailand, Indonesia, Fiji and New Zealand.

Normally stays in a country/city for: Less than one month.

Makes a living as a: Freelancer.

Meet Raven

I am a remote social media assistant for a few clients. I also dog-walk/house-sit when I am in an area longer than a few days. More recently, my travel blog (lattesnluggage.com) has been getting more traction, allowing me to sell travel itineraries and blog posts in exchange for free travel.

How Raven got started

It started in 2020, when I planned to take a gap year and backpack Europe. We all know how 2020 ended; I never did get to Europe. I got locked down in the USA. In that year, I did six weeks of road tripping the country, two weeks with a friend, two with my mother and two alone. In those two weeks alone, I ended up in Los Angeles for the first time, the place that I am currently calling my home. Here, I had extra time to build my website and brand and in my three months working at a beach cafe, I ran into a famous artist, who simply said, 'I want to hire you.' I quit my barista job, and became her assistant. I've worked for her in El Salvador, the Bahamas, Portugal, Paris, even in Iceland. It doesn't matter where I am, as long as I get the job done. I realized that this beat whatever corporate career I had lined up after graduation. I had found true freedom. I was able to make my own schedule, be wherever I wanted to be whenever, and still afford the expensive city of Los Angeles.

Raven's 'typical day'

You are completely right in saying there's no typical day. I suppose, currently, my days start with waking up and walking a dog. Whether I am house-sitting at this dog's home or driving over to an owner who is at work and walking their dog for them, this is part of my day. After the walk, I'll go home, workout, shower and hop on my laptop. If there were priorities in projects needing to be done today, I'd hammer those out. If not, I'd move onto more ambitious tasks: writing blog posts, scheduling social media or editing videos. If I'm not feeling creative, then I know it's time for a switch up in the routine and I'll pull up Skyscanner. Of the cheapest flight options, whichever destination I haven't been to yet, I'll book and start planning that trip. I find this is where the excitement lies. At around 5 or 6 p.m., my partner will get home from his job and we'll have dinner or drinks together, sharing our drama of the day, and then watch a movie before heading to bed.

Raven's favourite thing about the 'digital nomad' life is ...

Definitely the freedom that comes with it. I hate the idea that some people in life are allowed to have dreams and that others are just working for these people's dreams in a 9 to 5. I think everyone should have ambition and mine is to see the world, romanticize my life. I love being able to wake up and decide what I want to do for the day.

Her least favourite thing about the 'digital nomad' life is ...

Probably the uncertainty of my expenses. I may make five times more than rent this month, then break even the next. Since I freelance, I am constantly on this rollercoaster of ups and downs in my bank account, not knowing where it will end up.

Though I have savings I can always dip into, I wish I had more of a stable growth to depend on.

The number one thing Raven wished she knew when she first started out as a digital nomad is ...

It takes time to become known. If I could go back, I would've taken my side hustles more seriously. If I had done this, my website and clients would've been tenfold what they are now. Since I waited to truly respect this side of my ambition as more than just fun, I am just beginning to see the wonderful results. Had I not waited, I would've been on this career path during the pandemic when I had all the time in the world.

~~~~~~

5

Branding:
Be known as the go-to person in your space

~~~

Today, as I was working on this book, I was also involved in writing and content strategy assignments for:

» an American film producer for whom I'm editing a draft of a script we worked on together

» an American/Spanish education company for which I'm working on a round of edits for website copy

» a German cybersecurity company which is looking for content marketing support, and may or may not go on to become a full-time client.

All three of these companies came to me. The first, through personal connections in Poznan. The second two through LinkedIn. Networking and personal branding are overused terms. They bring to mind the agony of handshakes and business cards, cringe-worthy self-promotion, spamming friends on Facebook and pestering family members for business. But that's what these things look like when they're done wrong. Here's what networking and branding look like when it's done right: You have a specific skill and a service to offer (see Chapter 3). You know what this skill or service is, and you have a decent idea of the kinds of people who will benefit from it. Then, you set about establishing this so people know about it.

In the chapter on clients (see p. 68), we spoke about the three-step process of determining what value you provide, announcing this to the world, and tracking and proving this to your clients. Here, we'll look at other ways to build your brand as a digital nomad with a skill to sell ... without being obnoxious!

Online personal branding for freelancers and creatives

You've probably been told that if you want to make it as a freelancer, writer, designer or creative, you need a 'personal brand'. Having this 'brand' will make it more likely that editors and employers will recognize your name in their crowded inboxes and give your pitch, resume or application more attention. It will mean that instead of constantly chasing after commissions and sending out cold emails, commissions will come to you. Soon, you'll be carefully selecting the opportunities and clients that are most exciting (and financially rewarding), while turning down others.

That all sounds amazing, but how do you 'create' this coveted brand? Looking specifically at my own field of travel writing provides a useful lens through which to examine the challenges that all freelancers face. Jobs at 'legacy' media organizations, such as newspapers and magazines, are few and closely guarded. Even independent publications like *Intrepid Times* are drenched in submissions, meaning that getting published and building an audience can seem like a daunting process. Writers are told that without this so-called 'brand' they are unlikely to get serious publishers returning their emails. They are also told that in order to build this brand, you need to start getting published. This is like first being told that to climb a mountain you need hiking boots, only to find out that the remaining pair of hiking boots in your size are waiting for you at the top of the mountain! So, what do you do?

Regardless of what kind of freelancer (or even remote worker) you are, there are concrete steps you can take to create and build your personal brand, increase your perceived value and make it vastly easier for you to attract the kind of work that you want. And you don't even need to be a self-promoting extrovert to pull it off!

What is a freelancer's personal brand?

Your personal brand is a promise to a client that you can do the job they want. For example, your personal brand as a travel writer is a promise to an editor, publisher or client. When they see your name, the editor should know, thanks to your brand, that you:

» have a track record of delivering stories, designs or creative work on time (i.e. you won't mess with their editorial calendar)

» have proven expertise in the field that you are working in, for example in the subject matter you want to write on or the language you wish to code in

» have an audience in place of people who like and follow your work (i.e. the story they pay you for will have a ready-made readership in place). This applies especially for creatives.

But how do you build this personal brand, really?

For many new freelancers, this seems like an unsolvable 'chicken and egg' riddle. You build a brand by writing consistently for reputable publications, and using the attention these pieces get to build a social media presence. You get these gigs for reputable publications on the strength of your personal brand. But … if you are currently sitting at the beginning of your writing career without an industry reputation, where do you start?

Create a lot, and create often

While great writers, musicians and artists may be remembered for one or two iconic works, nearly every creative successful person (with some exceptions) was incredibly prolific. They produced, produced and produced. And the good thing about writing is that, unlike designing buildings or hewing marble into sculpture, you don't need a patron or budget to begin. Just start writing. Publish on platforms such as Medium, LinkedIn or WordPress, or your personal website.

Tell people about your work

No one likes a spammer, but if you're sharing genuinely useful helpful content, you're not doing anyone any harm. Get on Twitter (perhaps bad for your mental health, but good for making connections with editors and writers) and consider starting a Facebook fan page. Both are free. And then share consistently and often.

Share strategically to build relationships

Share your own works, and also the works of others in your space whom you admire. Don't bother with the huge names with ten million followers. Instead, interact with and share the content of writers just a few steps further along in the game than you. Folks with a few thousand followers will generally notice if their content is shared, and may reciprocate. Interact this way with the publications you admire, and they may start to recognize your name. Then when you start pitching to them, you won't be just another stranger in the inbox.

Define a (more specific) niche

While many creatives are generalists, those who make names for themselves quickly are typically specialists. For example, if you're a travel writer, you could specialize either in a region, or a style of travel. Many good niches are a combination of both. You could be the next dog friendly travel expert in Britain or Georgia food travel expert. Notice how both combine a regional specialization with a particular travel focus or style. Georgia is a reasonably underknown country for Western travellers, while food themes are, of course, very popular. Britain is a fairly popular travel destination, while dog friendly trips (one I imagine aimed mostly at the domestic traveller) is a little more niche.

If you were a travel writer, you could ask yourself these questions to help define your niche:

» Do you travel in a particular way that is notable or exceptional? For example, with children or a specific pet? (Cat friendly travel? Who knows, it might just be the next big thing.)

» Do you have a particular passion or field of expertise that could be applied to travel? Anthony Bourdain is the classic example of a chef bringing his culinary knowledge to bear on his travels and using food as a way to get to know a place better. Maybe you're a literary fanatic and can write about the literary history of a place. Or the architecture. This doesn't need to be something grand or high level. You could be the Parcheesi-playing travel expert if that suits your fancy!

» What places have drawn you in that you feel may be overlooked in most travel writing, but have potential? Thailand is probably overdone ... That said, the way the tourist industry is emerging from the pandemic may reveal something that others aren't yet covering. You probably already know if there's a particular place or region that pulls you back time and time again. Survey the landscape and connect with the established writers in those places using the social media strategies above. And ask yourself: is there something else you could bring to the table?

The same way of thinking applies to all creative fields. It's about finding the special way you design or create, and what defines the particular people you design or create for. And you need to hit the sweet spot between specific interest and broad appeal, provided there are actually people out there who are interested in this. The United States travel expert? Too broad. The Southwest Brooklyn Vegan Burrito travel expert? Too specific. Find something in between that is consistent with your interests. Soon, you may find yourself the go-to person in that space.

Personal branding for introverts

It might be natural to think that branding, even if done tastefully, is just for the entrepreneur or the freelancer. But even if your sights are set on having one stable employer for the long term while working remotely, a strong personal brand can make you more valuable to that particular organization and more hirable in the event that you (or they) decide it's time you got back on the job market.

While most of the tools of branding — websites, social media profiles, etc. — are public in nature, having a strong brand does not mean that you have to become an exhibitionist. You can have a strong brand in your circle, even if only a handful of people have heard of you.

This 'dark' reputation (dark in the sense of underground, as opposed to the sense of sinister or negative) can be sufficient to propel you to an interesting career on the road. It just requires you to have a very clear and specific sense of who you would like to work for. It's one thing being a freelance editor. It's another being a freelance script editor. And it's another being a freelance horror movie script editor. The more niche you are, the more private and focused your branding can be. You're taking the approach of a sniper as opposed to a grenade thrower.

Once you have a clear sense of exactly who you want to work for, set about researching them. LinkedIn is a great tool for this, so having a profile into which you've put a bit of effort can help your credibility when reaching out. Search for people with the keywords related to your super-specialization (i.e. horror-film script writer) and get a sense of the projects they're working on. Then reach out in a highly targeted way to offer your specialist services.

Research will be your friend and ally here. Learn as much as you can about the target client and the specific projects they are working on, and then suggest a next step that will allow them to see your value. Here's an example of how this could work.

> Subject line: Help with Nomad Zombies movie
>
> Hi [insert client name]
>
> I'm a big fan of your work, especially *Digital Nomads Gone Bad* and *Attack of the Vampire Backpackers*, and am very excited about the release of your work-in-progress, *Nomads Gone Bad*. I'm a professional script editor specializing in the horror genre, and would love to help you save time by offering my editorial services. You can learn more about me at [insert your link]. Let me know if you're free next week to chat about your project?
>
> Happy writing,
>
> [Your name]

Let's dissect the example above:

» It's about the client, not about you.

» It shows you've done your research.

» It makes a simple claim about the help you can provide and why they should care (in this case, saving them time).

» It provides a link to your profile so they can verify your credentials.

» It has a simple call to action, i.e. the next steps you want them to take to move forward.

This approach certainly won't have a 100 per cent success rate. But if you research ten prospective clients per day for a month during down-times in your day job, and sharpen your approach and offer through each interaction? Then by the end of the month it's not unrealistic to think that you're going to have a few clients in your pocket and the beginnings of a business that you can take with you wherever you go.

Branding for extroverts

Many of my best opportunities have arisen from the combination of three simple facts:

1. I've been part of a small, defined community of nomads, expats and locals.

2. I've had a clear skill that is in-demand among this community (i.e. writing and editing in English, a second language for most others in my circle).

3. People have known about this.

When you travel, you'll find a few things are inevitable. You can find good Wi-Fi in surprising locations (try five bars of reception at Mount Everest base camp in Tibet). McDonald's is a perfectly legitimate escape for a meal or two when your system just needs something familiar. And expats and nomad types are pretty much everywhere.

Hop onto Facebook, Meetup.com or Couchsurfing and find groups and meetups in your area. Show up, introduce yourself, and people will ask what you do. Conversations will lead to connections, and connections will often eventually become clients.

Your approach to this needs to be a mixture of subtle and bold. No one likes a flashy person who is clearly only there to 'hustle' and sees people as resources. On the other hand, if you are so humble that you never mention what you do, you'll never be able to find people whom you can genuinely help with your skillset.

The best attitude to take is one of 'I'm here to make friends and meet people and have fun. And if someone happens to be in need of [service I sell], then I'll be doing them a favour by letting them know.'

All meetup groups have different vibes, and some are more business focused than others. As you practise and show up more and more often, you'll learn how to read the room. Patience is valuable here: it may take time before enough trust is established to align your relationship into a fruitful business partnership. Be willing to start small. For example, a lot of my current clients have begun by asking for my help with something simple such as editing an article they had written, ghostwriting a travel story or proofreading a web page. Once people realize your value through this initial interaction, they will likely come back to you for more services. And then you can negotiate a retainer or a fixed fee. But none of this will happen if you aren't willing to put yourself out there in the first place!

The secret: Consistent action over time

You may get your 'niche' wrong at first. Observe closely what works and what doesn't. Adapt your approach. Be willing to follow unusual avenues if they seem to deliver results. Then you can refine your niche based on the kinds of projects that get results for you. The only guaranteed solution is consistent effort over time. So keep going!

MEET THE NOMADS

Name: Barrington Kirkham

Mid-thirties, from the UK.

Mostly travels: Alone or with friends.

Currently in: Edinburgh, Scotland, Poznan (Poland).

Digital nomad experience: Several years.

Has lived/worked/travelled in: The USA, Brazil, Poland, Australia and the UK.

Normally stays in a country/city for: A month or so.

Makes a living as an: Entrepreneur.

Meet Barrington

I am the founder of branding and digital marketing agency, fireflynewmedia.com, with clients globally. We began as a local magazine in Consett, North East England. I honed my skills in marketing and design, and built a network of professionals who could help. We started working for local businesses, mostly solving their digital problems, websites and such, before word of mouth started spreading. Now, we have clients the world over and team members in several countries too.

How Barrington got started

My journey as a nomad or 'entrepreneur who can't sit still' began back in 2014 when I visited Poland and worked remotely on expanding my marketing business, quickly realizing it was easily possible to work and travel at the same time. There really wasn't a name for remote working back then. COVID-19 hadn't happened yet and I wasn't aware of the 'digital nomad' term; however, without realizing it, I was indeed doing just that: remotely working as a digital nomad, travelling and working from airports, airplanes and Airbnb.

Barrington's 'typical day'

Wake, eat breakfast and drink a massive cup of coffee (on a nice balcony in the sun or overlooking the beach preferably), triple S (shit, shower, shave), write down what I want to get done today. I don't check my messages or emails before I prioritize my 'to-do' list, otherwise you can quite easily get sucked into other people's problems and your important tasks can be sidelined in a hurry. After planning my day without distractions (in a written journal or notepad), I smash some of the most difficult tasks first.

Take a break and have lunch. Go for a walk in a new part of town or at a cafe nearby to take in the vibes of the city or area that I'm currently in. At this stage I am still clear-headed without email distractions. If somebody really wants to get in touch with me they will call me or one of my team and let me know. Nothing in my inbox is really ever urgent — as long as I get to glance over it once or twice every 24 hours. Only when my priority tasks are done will I check emails.

In the afternoon I deal with any explosions in the email inbox, and make important phone calls (pacing on the balcony or walking outside, location and weather permitting). In the evening have a meal and a beer in a nice location, preferably with good company and interesting conversation.

Barrington's favourite thing about the 'digital nomad' life is ...

Being free and able to explore new places or, in two words: 'be inspired'.

His least favourite thing about the 'digital nomad' life is ...

Living out of a suitcase, packing, unpacking.

The number one thing Barrington wished he knew when he first started out as a digital nomad is ...

Get out of your comfort zone ASAP and never become complacent (go to new places, try new things, meet new people).

6

Negotiating:
Earn what you're worth and don't get penalized for travelling

~~~

Some nomads are happy to take the financial hit compared to earning a 'traditional' income, in exchange for the freedom that comes with the lifestyle. Others (including several you will meet in the interviews throughout this book) have decided to have both. And yes, it is possible to do so. But it takes time, and the willingness to sacrifice a little bit. You may be forcing your groggy head up early in the morning so you can smash out work before going sightseeing. You may be up until the wee hours on Zoom calls with clients in multiple time zones as opposed to hitting the famous local bars.

There's a lot of talk out there about nomads who work a few hours per week and make hundreds of thousands a year. But of the small percentage of those who are actually telling the truth, you bet there were years when they worked sixteen-hour days in order to build the relationships, profile and pipelines that got them to where they are now. A few may have got lucky betting on one cryptocurrency or another, but luck is not a reliable strategy. You can wait around for it forever. Or you can pack your laptop and hit the road.

We've spoken about some strategies to onboard clients. And once you have them, you're going to want to get paid. And this means you're going to need to negotiate a price for your services.

This aspect has been one of the areas of the digital nomad life I have most struggled with. Advice online steered me strongly towards trying to charge big dollars in the early days, before I had an established reputation to fall back on. I then overcompensated for some years, working below the rates I could secure in order to keep work coming in, and have only recently found some kind of equilibrium. The key for me has been having an abundance of clients, built over time using a mixture of the branding and client acquisition strategies described in the previous chapters.

The process of establishing clients snowballs and, like London buses, you find that after you've waited months for a particular client, they all come at once. Once you're mature enough in your branding and expertise and clients are coming to you regularly, you can negotiate from a position of strength, knowing that if this particular prospect says no, there will be plenty of others waiting in the wings. I recently turned down a client who asked me to lower the rates I had quoted for them. I politely but firmly declined, and they came back to me accepting my original offer. This is a good position to be in, but it's taken me the better part of a decade to get here!

Along the way I have made (and continue to make) a number of mistakes that have clipped the wings of my earning potential. As I work to resolve this now, there are a few pieces of advice I wish I had heard years ago that may also help you.

» Be flexible. Charging per word, by the hour, by article, by month? I currently use a variation of all of these different arrangements depending on the client, their needs and the type of relationship I have with them. Especially in your early days, being willing to adapt and have flexible practices can set you apart from the competition because it makes you easier to work with. As your reputation grows and the power dynamic between you and potential clients shifts, you can make more demands and fewer concessions.

» Know your value. But how? The market rate of services, particularly in the creative space, is murky at the best of times and has been greatly warped by platforms such as Fiverr which claim to deliver professional services for next to nothing. You can combat this by gathering data from alternative sources. Platforms such as Glassdoor and Indeed, for example, publish average hourly rates for most professions. From this, you can extrapolate a rough freelance rate for your services, and you can use this data to back yourself up in client negotiations.

» Be prepared to say no … (sometimes). Yes, clichéd advice, but it bears repeating because it is so easy to panic and ignore it. I've certainly had experiences when I've worked well below my rates. Sometimes, these experiences have actually been worth it in the long run because I've created pieces that I could add to my portfolio, sharpened my skills and business knowledge, and gained a useful client endorsement. So, my qualification would be 'Be prepared to say no … unless you know what you're getting'.

» Don't listen to advice. Except this! Even here, take everything with a backpack full of salt. Memes in the creative spaces abound, mocking those jobs that pay you in 'exposure'. Certainly exploitation of freelancers and creatives is rampant, but being over sensitive to this can actually obscure real opportunities. It is legitimate, especially when starting out, to assign more than a simple dollar amount to the value of a particular gig.

» Frame your worth in a way that's compelling. As we've explored elsewhere, people want to know the impact you can have on their life and business. Go a layer deeper, and think about how the life of your client is better thanks to you. Do they have more time, less stress, more income, less expenses? Train your clients to see you as an investment rather than an expense by reminding them of the value you provide, and you'll drastically unlock your earning potential.

» Form partnerships. With clients whose businesses are at an early stage, consider taking a risk and accepting a lower fee in exchange for a profit share. This is exciting because it means your work is going towards something that you share an ownership stake in, and it can unlock the potential for exponential gains in the long run.

Low-paid freelancers are hesitant about their value, anxious about which offers to take, and apologetic about their fees. High-paid freelancers are willing to say no, are confident in the value they bring to their clients and able to form long-term partnerships with exponential upsides. It's a long (and rocky) road, and one that I am still learning how to navigate. But time is on your side. The longer you have been doing this, the more clients or potential clients you will know, the weightier your portfolio, and the better your understanding of what the market wants. Persist, adapt and learn and, as the evidence of many nomads who have contributed interviews to this book shows, you could unlock an earning potential while hopping the globe that is at least the equal of your peers who chose the sedentary life.

~~~~~~

MEET THE NOMADS:

Name: Enrique Hygge

Late-twenties, from the US.

Mostly travels: Half the time alone, half the time with his partner.

Currently in: The Netherlands.

Digital nomad experience: Several years.

Has lived/worked/travelled in: China, Austria, Denmark and the United States.

Normally stays in a country/city for: A month or so.

Makes a living as an: Entrepreneur.

Meet Enrique

I design, manufacture and sell widgets directly to consumers all around the world at [redacted].com. Originally, I founded and ran the business alone, but now we have a small, fully remote team. While work does take me back to the United States sometimes, especially when we have widgets that need shipping out the door, the majority of the work can be done anywhere.

How Enrique got started

One week after graduating from university I flew to China on a one-way ticket with $500 to my name and $10,000 in student loan debt in search of opportunity. With ambitions fuelled by unbridled confidence and naivete, my plan was to enter a hyper-saturated market with zero experience and figure things out along the way. In short — questionable decision making paired with an intense desire to succeed.

Enrique's 'typical day'

Show up to a local library around 10 a.m. and work there until 4 p.m. while consuming copious amounts of coffee and listening to a YouTube livestream of 'Lofi Hip Hop Beats to Relax/ Study To'. Glamorous to say the least.

Enrique's favourite thing about the 'digital nomad' life is ...

Living in a state of constant fear that I'll fuck everything up and end up having to live like the majority of society. On the face of it, this may come across as rather depressing, but I find it motivating as it reminds me of how thankful I am to be doing what I do each day.

His least favourite thing about the 'digital nomad' life is ...

Packing. Jet lag. Dubious Airbnb accommodations. Customs and border control. Travel days. The realization that working from a laptop on the beach is really only possible when doing it for a staged Instagram post.

The number one thing Enrique wished he knew when he first started out as a digital nomad is ...

Nothing. Throw yourself into the abyss and take every day as it comes.

7

Employers:

How to seek stability
even when travelling
long-term

~~~

The freelance option is appealing for many nomads who want independence. It means you're never overly reliant on any one particular company. You can set your own hours, disappear when you need to, and enjoy the variety of working with different companies who will bring you different challenges.

There is also appeal in getting a 'traditional' full-time job, albeit one that lets you work on the road. Advantages to this kind of job can include:

» Security. You know what you're getting paid this month and the month after, and you may also enjoy additional benefits.

» Advancement. If climbing the corporate ladder appeals to you, then you best start by getting yourself on the ladder.

» Set hours. Your contract will likely say when you're working and when you're not, so no clients blowing up your phone in the middle of the night.

» Community. Freelancing can be lonely, so working in a company can provide you with a sense of community, and more and more fully-remote companies are now sponsoring occasional in-person meetups for their teams.

It used to be that jobs in the information space were in offices. But that is changing at a rapid rate. Spurred on by the pandemic, remote or hybrid work opportunities are on the rise like never before. The website Findstack.com reports that already 16 per cent of the world's companies are 100 per cent remote, and that remote workers actually earn more on average than others.

If the idea of working remotely from around the world appeals to you, then you have two options: find a remote job, or transition your current office job to a remote position. Let's look at both.

Finding a remote job

Many of the steps we outlined in the previous chapter, including defining your value proposition, setting up an attractive LinkedIn page and networking in a way that adds value will also serve you well when looking for a remote job. The fact is, many companies now don't care where you are as long as you have the skills that they are looking for.

That said, I've also come across many companies who:

» will hire remote workers, but want to meet them in person first during the interview stage

» will hire remote workers, but only hire in their own country (i.e. Americans to do remote work in the United States)

» will hire based on a hybrid model, meaning you can work remotely for a certain set of days.

Some companies allocate their employees a fixed number of days specifically for working overseas. Others will specify a time zone that you need to be active in (whether or not this corresponds to you being a vampire in your actual location may or may not be their concern!).

Options abound, so first have a think and decide what you are going for: 100 per cent remote, or some form of compromise. Then search on websites like Indeed.com for jobs that suit your expectations. You may want to play the long game if you aren't yet qualified for jobs which combine good pay with the remote prospects that you want. Write down the qualifications or experience you are lacking, and work towards gaining them. Any experience you can gain with clients as a full- or part-time employee can actually help position you well for a full-on remote career, and in my work I've taken on quasi 'formal' roles with clients when I've been in their time zone, not only for the increased income for a fixed time, but also for the interaction and experience of working with a team, which is something you can miss as a freelancer.

Working for a corporation on a part-time basis, combined with freelancing or a side hustle (see the next chapter on page 115) can be a great way to balance stability with growth and independence as you first venture out into the world, untethered.

Transitioning to remote nomadic work

If you already work in an office job and you believe you have a shot at becoming a 'digital nomad' without losing your paycheck, then here are some tips for making the case. First, establish precedent. Chances are your company was fully remote, at least for a time, during the pandemic. You probably put systems in place that allowed you to remain productive during this time. Give examples of projects you delivered under remote conditions. This will build confidence that the work will still be done, even when you're overseas.

Next, explain your wishes in the context of personal development: Make it clear that your intention is not to backpack, moving every three days and getting drunk. You wish to develop yourself as a person through exposure to other cultures. If anything, this will make you a more creative and helpful team member, as you will bring new and interesting perspectives to the team.

Finally, test the waters. It's easier for people to say 'yes' to things with very defined scope. Start by asking if you can work remotely, say, for one month. And then, if that is successful, you could ask for more opportunities to do so. Eventually, your employers will realize that you working remotely is not a threat to them at all.

The 'in-the-room' advantage

There's a fear that taking the remote route, even if permitted by your employer, may put you at a relative disadvantage with your colleagues who show up on a permanent or hybrid basis in the office. And there's certainly truth here, as while Zoom calls can go a long way towards bridging communication divides across distances, it's not the same as the relaxed, cross-functional spontaneity that can occur in an office environment.

You can minimize this disadvantage in a couple of ways. First, create opportunities to show up in person occasionally. Even an occasional face-to-face meeting can make a huge difference. With a long-term remote client who employs people on a hybrid basis, I recently volunteered to help out at one of their upcoming conferences. While I didn't need to be there in order to do my writing job for them, I wagered that seizing the opportunity to meet colleagues in the company in-person would help cement relationships and increase my knowledge of the company and its customers. Making this happen a couple of times a year (spending 'quality time' with your colleagues and bosses, if you will) can change how you are seen in the business.

Another general best-practice habit especially important for remote workers — and that we also speak about in the context of negotiating pay as a freelancer — is to track your efforts and results. Often 'individual contributors' (i.e. people who actually write code or copy or do things on a daily basis, as opposed to managers) assume their efforts are noticed, but actually people in higher up roles may be oblivious to what you largely do. Keeping notes and tracking your results can help you secure your employment and also put you in a much stronger position to negotiate for extras, including a pay rise or the freedom to work from anywhere.

Remote work is becoming more acceptable by the day. If you want to keep your job while seeing the world, then this could be your moment. It's an opportunity that, still, remarkably few people seem to realize is available for them. Take the opportunities while they are there!

~~~~~~~~~~~~~~~~~~~~~~~~~~~~~~~~~

MEET THE NOMADS

Name: Sarah Cash

American, mid-thirties.

Mostly travels: Alone, but often meets up with friends.

Currently in: Oxford, UK.

Digital nomad experience: Over eight years.

Has lived/worked/travelled in: France, Switzerland, Jamaica, New Zealand, Greece, Portugal, Croatia, Brazil, Argentina, UK, Spain, Vietnam, Australia, Turkey and Malta.

Normally stays in a country/city for: Two or three months.

Makes a living as a: Remote worker.

Meet Sarah

I work in travel for point.me, helping people book flights with points and use credit cards to maximize their point earnings. They let all employees work from wherever they want as long as they work when the customer is available, which is usually US hours. I travel to different locations based on a few factors: conferences I might join, family events, joining friends to travel and simply going to places I want to. Also, I try not to travel too fast but rather stay in one region for a while. I've been in Europe since March, and I'll go back to the Americas in September to be with my family.

How Sarah got started

I've been living out of the US off and on since I was seventeen. That's when I studied abroad in France and became hooked on experiencing other cultures. Since then I've attended university, served in the Peace Corps, backpacked from Bulgaria to Australia, and lots of other weird and wonderful things, but I've never stopped being fascinated by travel and the opportunities it unfolds.

Now I work remotely from wherever, helping travellers maximize their spending by educating them on the best way to earn and spend credit card points. I love the flexibility of being able to choose where I call home and for how long. There are definitely days when it gets tiring or lonely, but it's worth all the challenges.

Sarah's 'typical day'

A typical day looks different depending on the time zone but if I'm in Africa or Europe, I have the morning to myself. I'll get up, take a walk or work out, and maybe visit a local attraction like the beautiful gardens in England where I am currently. I tend to cook more when I'm on my own but I also love eating new foods, whether it's Michelin-starred restaurants or food stalls. In the afternoon I'll start working, mostly talking to clients or coworkers over Zoom. On the weekend I might go for a hike, see a local play or just Netflix and chill; it really depends on where I am and how I'm feeling. Digital nomads: we're just like you!

Sarah's favourite thing about the 'digital nomad' life is ...

The freedom and getting to know different cultures around the world. The simple satisfaction I feel knowing I can truly work from anywhere (where there's Wi-Fi) is hard to oversell. I value independence more than most so I'm living my dream! The travel aspect is equally life-changing. I can taste tacos in Mexico rather than just visiting a Mexican restaurant abroad. The experiences I have are difficult to replicate, and I'm so grateful.

Her least favourite thing about the 'digital nomad' life is ...

When you travel too quickly, you can burn out. There are definitely times when I arrive in a place I've never visited but all I want to do is sit and do nothing for a few days. I think it's very important to recognize your energy level and work to replenish it, rather than force a situation. If I want to be a homebody and not take a bus, plane, train, camel etc., for two weeks, I do that until I feel that curiosity to explore returning.

On that note, creating routines for yourself is critical so that when a once-in-a-lifetime opportunity comes up, you have the presence and desire to deviate from your norm.

The number one thing Sarah wished she knew when she first started out as a digital nomad is ...

You don't need to plan too much. Like any lifestyle, you'll figure it out as you go. This is probably more true for those who tend to overplan. Go ahead, watch all the YouTube digital nomad videos and read all the blogs, but when it comes down to it, you'll find your own rhythm and adjust accordingly. The beauty of this lifestyle is how adaptable it is; if you don't want to stay in a place for as long as you planned, you don't have to!

On a different but related note, I wish more people emphasized that you can travel with debt. I have student loans, but using geo-arbitrage (earning money in an expensive country and spending it in a cheaper one), I save money that I can put towards that. It would take me longer to pay off my debt if I only lived in the US.

8

Entrepreneurs:
What it takes to build a business that can fund your travels

~~~

If getting a remote job with a stable corporation is the most stable way to make a living as you travel the world, entrepreneurship may be the hardest and the most exciting. There's a couple of reasons why this book is not fully focused on the idea of being an entrepreneur as you travel the world. One is that the subject has been done to death, and you'll struggle to find a potential digital nomad who has not read *The 4-Hour Workweek* by Tim Ferris. Another is that, despite the boosterism of authors with books or courses to sell on how easy it is to become an entrepreneur, the truth is that most businesses fail. That's true no matter how many books you read about how easy it is. Starting a successful business requires certain abilities which I believe are innate: you either have them or you don't. Some of these are:

» Strategic intuition. You can figure out new and creative ways to build things and solve problems that others have not considered.

» Courage. You're going to be fully responsible not just for your own income but also for any employees you may have. You may risk your life savings, or go into debt in pursuit of your dreams.

» Passion. But not necessarily passion for your product, but passion specifically for the process. You have to love the grind, or you will not do it.

» Charm. Business leaders persuade others, whether it's customers or investors, to go along with their vision for something new.

Without at least a healthy dose of most of the above, I don't think entrepreneurship is the right path. And that's okay: you don't have to be an entrepreneur to live an amazing life! You don't have to start a business to achieve financial independence. You don't have to invent your own product in order to make a profit and travel the world. Being a freelancer is a perfectly good and respectable option. As is being a remote worker. But if entrepreneurship is in your blood then it's unlikely that these words of caution will dissuade you. In fact, you're probably feeling defiant and more motivated than ever!

Untethered does not set out to be a comprehensive guide to digital entrepreneurship. And while much of the advice in previous chapters about positioning, setting expectations and networking is relevant for entrepreneurs, starting businesses also presents many unique challenges that there simply is not space to go into here. Therefore, I will simply outline a strategy that I've found personally rewarding, which may help you decide whether or not entrepreneurship is for you.

The side hustle

A side hustle is a tiny business you start as outside of your job or your freelance career. Typically, side hustles are:

» bootstrapped and require little to no investment, so you don't need to have capital to get started

» niche and targeted to a small, passionate group of people or a small dedicated community rather than mass-market

» scalable in that, if it takes off, then it may become your 'main hustle,' but it will still be considered a success if it stays on the side

» generally solo projects or started with a very small team of partners, where typically one person will wear every hat, creating the product and doing the marketing and customer service, at least at the start.

Side hustle example: *Intrepid Times*

While it now forms a major part of my business and work life, the travel writing publication *Intrepid Times* originally started off as something of a classic side hustle. It began as a vehicle for publishing my own travel writing and interviewing my favourite travel authors. The set-up costs were negligible, just a website registered through GoDaddy, hosting with Siteground, and maybe a splurge of a couple of hundred dollars for a designer on Freelancer. com to create the logo.

My plan was to grow my freelance copywriting business on the one hand, doing my 'commercial' or paid work for a range of clients on a freelance- and remote-work basis. And with the other, I would build *Intrepid Times* by consistently posting quality content, making relationships with people in the travel space who had audiences and supported what we were doing, and evolving the platform into something that other writers could find their own space on.

As I started publishing other travel writers from around the world, I noticed there were a large number of aspiring travel writers who had stories they were eager to tell, but lacked the foundational writing knowledge needed to convey their stories in a punchy and publishable manner. I started offering online writing courses which finally made *Intrepid Times* another income stream for my business.

This side hustle is a little unusual in the case that it started out as a passion project and I always knew it would take a number of years before it became a profitable venture. This is true also of a number of podcasters and bloggers. If profit is your core motive (and there's no reason why it shouldn't be), then the calculations are a little different. You're going to have to take more risks, work long hours, and constantly iterate and adapt.

From the entrepreneurs you will encounter in these pages, such as Nora Dunn to Enrique Hygge, you'll notice that their paths are radically different. Enrique Hygge was willing to gamble everything to make his widget business work. Nora sold her successful financial planning business and spent her life savings to start travelling. It worked out for them, but many other entrepreneurs failed along the way. This is why I advocate a dual, incremental approach. Work on transitioning remotely with your employer or freelance business, while simultaneously building a bootstrapped side hustle in an area that aligns, at least somewhat, with your interests or passions. If you are successful, your side hustle will eventually become your main hustle. And if not, you haven't sacrificed your opportunities for freedom, nor wasted time and energy on something that you are not congruent with. And certainly you'll learn a lot in the pursuit of your side hustle that will make you more effective and not to mention more employable — many hiring managers specifically look out for side hustles on resumes because it shows initiative and drive.

All these options for making money while on the road as a digital nomad may be making your head spin. So here's something that may help steady you — in order to live and travel overseas, you probably have to earn less money than you think. We will look at aspects of this in the next chapter.

MEET THE NOMADS

Name: Cathy Raymond

Mid-fifties, from the United States.

Mostly travels: I often travel/work/live abroad alone, but sometimes my husband or kids come along.

Currently in: St Louis, USA.

Digital nomad experience: Several years.

Has lived/worked/travelled in: Germany, Nepal, Afghanistan, Tajikistan, Uzbekistan and Russia.

Normally stays in a country/city for: Two or three months.

Makes a living as an: English teaching professional.

Meet Cathy

I have taught English professionally for over 35 years. I am passionate about learning new languages, meeting people from around the world and living in new countries. My work as an English teacher has allowed me to live and work in many different countries. I don't like visiting new countries as a tourist; I much prefer living and working with locals, so I can get to know new languages and cultures more deeply.

How Cathy got started

Many years ago, I got my MA in TESOL/Applied Linguistics in the US, and I have worked as an English teacher ever since. (I'm not a fan of the title 'English as a Second Language teacher' because most of the people I work with speak several languages, and English is often the fourth or fifth for them. It seems a bit presumptuous to me to tell them they are learning English as a 'second' language ...)

One of my first English teaching experiences was in an Intensive English Language Program in the USA. Those classrooms were filled to the brim with highly diverse students from all over the globe, and I quickly learned that our differences are a resource for rich and meaningful conversations about language, culture, tradition, family and passion. Over time, I also gradually started developing courses in culture, short stories and creative writing. Students forged connections to each other as they journalled about their individual experiences as creative readers and writers, and we published creative writing journals at the end of each semester.

I have always identified myself as a global citizen, so it was natural for my German husband and me to give our children international names and to raise them as world citizens. (They both just recently moved to Berlin — jealous!) I have been fortunate in my life to receive many jobs and grants for English teaching and educational research; these diverse opportunities have taken me on adventures all around the world, including to Germany, Nepal, Russia, Kazakhstan, Uzbekistan, Tajikistan and Afghanistan. (In the process, I have also become something of a 'Stan fan'!)

Cathy's 'typical day'

A typical day would be hard to describe, but it might include some variation of English teaching or research combined with a long mountain hike or a spontaneous conversation in Russian on a bus in Tajikistan with a very old woman wearing her dead husband's highly decorated military jacket. Or it might involve sitting on the floor around a *dastarkhan* (Turkish for tablecloth) piled high with a variety of meats, vegetables, warm bread, desserts, juice, berries and lots and lots of sweet treats.

Cathy's favourite thing about the 'digital nomad' life is ...

My favourite thing about living/working around the world is that I get to know new languages and cultures more deeply than if I were visiting as a tourist. I have colleagues and friends all over the world as a result.

**Her least favourite thing about
the 'digital nomad' life is …**

Some of the places I have lived have serious problems with water and/or air quality, and that can sometimes be physically challenging.

**The number one thing Cathy wished she knew
when she first started out as a digital nomad is …**

My international work life has been such an adventure and an amazing journey so far, and I'm glad to have learned much along the way. If I had known everything I needed to know, the journey would not have been so exciting!

9

Currency:

How to handle money, exchange rates, taxes and more

~~~

As I am writing *Untethered* in the third quarter of 2022, rampant inflation seems to be taking over the world. From the UK to New Zealand (and pretty much everywhere in between), weekly grocery shops are noticeably more expensive, rent is going up, and wages do not seem to be keeping pace.

Because of the uncertainty and the rapid pace of change, giving specific numbers for how much money you need to earn to live and travel the world does not seem wise. What I write today will be ancient history by the time this book reaches your hands. Therefore, I want to just paint some broad strokes covering the things you will need to pay for on the road, and some advice for handling them and saving along the way.

Some nomads obsess over this aspect of the life. They geek out on currencies and crypto, and apply astonishing amounts of creativity to save money on accommodation and travel, subscribing to various complex credit card reward systems, scouting out error fares, staying in communal accommodation or using work-for-stay arrangements. This has never been me. While I'm not extravagant and live fairly frugally, I've always preferred to apply my energies to the process of earning money rather than being particularly creative about saving. Especially since I generally enjoy my copywriting work and the people I work for. A more appealing equation for me is: work a little harder, earn a little more, and optimize for enjoyment and career/business growth rather than savings, point ordering, or frugality of lifestyle. This philosophy is the one that suits me, but I am not recommending it to everyone.

You may be the kind of person who is enthralled by exchange rates, or excited by the prospect of getting one over on the system and scoring an outrageously good deal and, if so, you will almost certainly find yourself going above and beyond the simple advice I lay out below. But hopefully this basic overview of how I, at least, manage the finances and expenses of a digital nomad lifestyle will help you organize your own thinking and decide where you choose to apply that extra dose of energy and creativity in your life.

Where you stay

Tools like Airbnb and Booking.com make it easy to find places to stay, but they charge high fees to homeowners which means that they are not always ideally suited for mid-term rental. When you're new to a city and not sure how long you want to stay for, going through the traditional apartment rental process is expensive and intimidating. So, what's the middle ground?

A formula that you might find effective is this: book a home (i.e. a privately owned apartment) on a service like Airbnb and pay there. Then, if you like the place and want to stay longer, make a private deal with the owner. You lose the protection that the Airbnb platform provides, so there is risk, but you also get the chance of a flexible, short-to- medium-term accommodation rental, normally around half the price a place may be listed for online. This formula has proven effective for me and other nomads I've spoken to across Europe, though I've yet to try it out myself in Asia.

How you get there

There's a bit of a movement going on right now against flying, for environmental reasons. While I am no fan of corporate polluters, I am generally pro-flying and against flight-shaming, for reasons I laid out quite extensively in my last book, *Travel Your Way: Rediscover the world on your own terms.* Tools like SkyScanner.net and Google Flights make it easy to find connections, and budget airlines like Europe's RyanAir and Asia's AirAsia provide seductively cheap international connections even at short notice.

If you're in Europe, ground transportation can be cheaper even than budget airlines. Train travel (book internationally anywhere in Europe though Germany's bahn.com/en) can provide great bargains and is also much more pleasant, in my opinion, than any other means. While not super comfortable, long distance bus travel with FlixBus can be astonishingly affordable. Particularly in Eastern Europe, ride sharing companies like BlaBlaCar can provide opportunities to travel internationally by private car.

How you spend

Different countries typically mean different currencies! There was a time when banks would relish punishing you for this fact by charging exorbitant fees for international transactions, and I'm told some still do. I have also faced problems with my home bank accounts blocking my cards for suspicious overseas transactions that were actually legit, and have ended up spending hours providing my identity to various bored call-centre operators. To avoid both these problems, I now use Wise.com (formerly known as TransferWise).

Their international accounts are designed for travellers and don't sting you on fees. Just make sure you always select the local currency whenever a terminal or ATM asks for your preference, otherwise they will try to profit off a rigged conversion rate.

How to stay safe and healthy

Travelling can be an enormous strain on the body, and unfamiliar foods and environments can lead to visits to local medical clinics. Most old-school travel insurance is designed for short trips and can be tricky for long-term travellers who do not know when (or even if) they will ever return home. Recently, however, insurance options have been cropping up optimized specifically for digital nomads. One such example is Safety Wing, which I use (and am not affiliated with other than being a customer). At the time of writing, I've not had to rely upon them for a claim (touch wood!) so I can't speak to that experience, but their communication and marketing is clearly aimed at nomad types like me.

Otherwise travel insurance options abound, and many will cover long-term travel. Taking out a policy with a company based in your home country may be much cheaper than this. And if you already have a health insurance policy at home, it's possible that it may cover your expenses abroad too, within certain time periods. Call your provider and ask: you may not even have to add anything extra!

How you stay in touch

Like bank fees, mobile phone roaming charges haunt the dreams of many a garrulous globetrotter. However, the situation seems to have improved, especially in Europe where SIM cards tend to work across borders. I have a long-term contract with EE that gives me roaming (within their 'fair use' policy), in the UK and EU and also places like Australia, New Zealand and the United States. My phone also has two SIM cards, so when I am living or travelling outside of these places for any length, I will buy a local SIM to cover the internet and calls during my stay, and typically all you need for this is a passport.

Some phones are also compatible with E-SIMs, which are basically an electronic SIM card that you can download. I have had the service Aairalo.com recommended to me; it offers E-sims for numerous countries as well as international packages. I am not affiliated with them and have not had the opportunity to test their services, but it may be worth looking into if you have an up-to-date smartphone and a certain comfort level with technology.

If all of this messing around with SIM cards is as daunting to you as it is to me, then you may not even need to do it. Before you go wandering, check with your current provider to see if they can move you to a plan with better roaming options. For shorter trips, you may also be able to get away with just using Wi-Fi access and placing calls over apps like WhatsApp or using something like Google Voice from your laptop.

How to stay tax compliant

As Mark Twain famously said, the only two certainties in life are death and taxes. Many digital nomads are uncertain about how to handle this tax aspect. Different countries have different rules, and a complete explanation of tax compliance for nomads would require a whole book, a tedious one that would inevitably be self-contradictory and quickly obsolete. From my understanding, it looks like most tax rules were written for a pre-internet age, where 'work' was something you did in person.

However, some countries are catching up, and googling 'digital nomad visa' will give you a few options for countries in Europe and the Caribbean, for example, which have visa arrangements specifically for digital nomads with tax compliance baked into the arrangements. Other countries offer generous tax terms for international residents and have attracted many nomads to adopt one of them as their 'home' for tax purposes. According to nomadgirl.co, 46 countries offer digital nomad visas as of 2022, including Croatia, Germany, Norway, Portugal, Barbados, Bermuda, the Cayman Islands, Anguilla, Montserrat and Dominica. Availability changes quickly as countries are still figuring out this new area, so if it is of interest to you, do your research in advance and find out what is available based on your citizenship and also where you want to live. While the Caymans are no doubt beautiful, I much prefer somewhere with a higher probability of a midnight train adventure to an unknown city.

Your best move will depend a lot on where you are from, as certain countries like the United States impose extra complexities upon their citizens. A good rule-of-thumb is that while countries will generally consider you a 'resident' for tax purposes if you stay there more than about six months in a given year, most countries also have a network of double tax treaties in place, meaning that if you have already paid tax for your income in country X, you may not actually have to pay it again in country Y, even if you've stayed there long enough to qualify. In addition, you should find out what the 'tax declaration threshold' is for the particular country you are in, as if you're earning modest sums you may not qualify for taxation anyway.

All of these problems only present themselves if you plan to stay somewhere for as much as six months (with a few exceptions like the United States, which does take itself rather seriously in this regard). Do your research on the tax codes wherever you happen to drop anchor, and check what thresholds and tax treaties may be in place. Accountants are increasingly accustomed to dealing with digital nomad types, and so you may be able to find more comprehensive advice specific to your situation.

Some of this has become easier thanks to the pandemic. Banks and governments have made it easier to handle certain bureaucratic procedures online or over the phone. Residency requirements in various places have been relaxed. But digital nomading is not an escape from all of the boring vicissitudes of adulthood. In many ways, it can make these challenges more complex, not less.

The nomad dilemma

Governments and institutions like simplicity. They want you to have a fixed, stable address; a fixed, stable income; and work for a fixed, stable company. Living everywhere, working as you travel and earning money from various sources does not fit the script.

Almost every nomad I know handles these problems differently. Some make it a passion to be as efficient as possible: obtaining tax residency in Georgia where rates are tantalizingly low; signing up for every fancy, remote bank account possible; forming connections with expat doctors and healthcare services in various countries. Others choose to ignore all of this completely. They dance between the raindrops, slipping under the radar, hoping that no government or health issue will ever catch up with them.

I suppose I fall somewhere in the middle. I maintain a limited company and sometimes spend quite painful sums of money on accountants and lawyers here and there to make sure I comply with laws and taxation needs at home and abroad. I have travel insurance that covers me wherever I go, as well as local health insurance for Poland, where I have been based for the last several months. For me, dealing with these problems is a source of anxiety and frustration. But ignoring them can result in consequences that can seriously cripple your freedom. I expect there will be two types of people reading this, so let me address each group in turn.

Tax and finance for 'life hackers'

You love figuring out how to (legally) game the system, finding the shortest route between A and B. New technology excites you, you are frequently an early adopter and probably even a cryptocurrency fan! If you truly plan to have no home, then finding a tax haven somewhere in Europe (Portugal and Georgia are popular options) or even the Caymans may be for you.

You are the type who will research all the ins and outs, arm yourself with numerous remote bank accounts, and probably create multiple companies in order to best optimize your tax exposure. You will look on expat forums in the destinations you are considering for accountants and tax advisers who can help you tick the boxes and do the needed paperwork. You may also obsess over services like Revolut and Wise (previously known as TransferWise) that can help you bank on the move.

Tax and finance 'technophobes'

When topics like international bank accounts, taxation, visas and residency come up, you probably melt into a puddle of anxiety. Take heart, the fact that the world isn't set up to accommodate the digital nomad kind also means it's not set up to 'detect' you. You aren't a criminal, and unless you're moving tens of thousands of dollars around, chances are no one really cares that you're earning some money from your blog or your remote job. Keep paying taxes wherever you currently pay them, and try not to brag too publicly when you have the occasional good month. Your bank card may cause you problems overseas, so getting a card through Wise, Revolut or N26 if you're in Europe really isn't a bad idea, and it's not that complex.

Nomads are not squares!

The world is not set up for digital nomads. You will fundamentally be a round peg living in a world full of squares. Recently, after two years of pandemic weirdness coupled with Brexit, life admin has taken up a larger chunk of my mental bandwidth than I would have wanted it to. I could have avoided some of these anxieties by being proactive with the steps I laid out above, and by more courageously embracing some of the 'life hack' solutions.

Ultimately, what I am learning to do is deal with these admin tasks as I would any mission from a client. It takes time and is annoying, but it's got to be done. If you are just starting out, I would recommend sorting out, at least to begin with, where you are storing your money and how you are spending it. If, like me, you first started travelling the world with the same local bank account your mother opened for you when you were five, this will cause problems when overseas transactions lead to your cards being frozen. A Wise card has saved many headaches here.

Reassure yourself also with the fact that few people really know what they are doing in this area. You can find millions of articles online about 'life hacking' or 'travel hacking' where people will extol the benefits of this card or that rewards system or this insurance program. Really, the daylight between these choices isn't likely to be that much. It's a decision you have to make about how much of your precious time and mental energy you want to put towards this aspect of the lifestyle. 'As little as possible without really fucking up' has been my general rule so far, a ratio that I haven't always got right. But if you enjoy optimizing your life and expenses and taxes and health care and all that jazz, you have certainly chosen the right lifestyle!

MEET THE NOMADS

Name: Harry Cunningham

New Zealander, in his late twenties.

Mostly travels: With his wife.

Currently in: London.

Digital nomad experience: Five years.

Has lived/worked/travelled in: Singapore, Australia, India, England, Scotland and New Zealand.

Normally stays in a country/city for: A month or so.

Makes a living as a: Remote worker.

Meet Harry

I lead a team of coaches and conduct coaching sessions (and team meetings) remotely. I also teach apprentices and create (and execute) team growth strategies.

How Harry got started

Since my first big overseas trip when I was fourteen, I was hooked on travel. My primary determinant for what I studied at university was 'does it have the word "international" in the title, and will it take me overseas?' In my first job, nine months in, I 'convinced' (tricked?) my employer to pay for a 'business' trip to India to train a team I was working with. Nine months later, I somehow wrangled a three-month excursion to live and work in Singapore, much to the disbelief of my fellow graduates on the same program as me. They were annoyed I was given the opportunity, but I was the only one who asked and, more importantly, made it happen.

Since then, I have lived my life from sabbatical to sabbatical, working hard for a few months to a year, then taking off a more significant period of time: three months, four months, six months. I am now based in the UK but I spend every other month in a different country, but still have that 'normal' career of a 9 to 5 regular salaried job with a single employer. In my view, you can do both: be a digital nomad with a steady secure job and a pension. With remote working, it is no longer a decision you always have to make.

Harry's 'typical day'

I work pretty standard hours of 9–5 p.m., but I can work from basically anywhere. When I am not abroad I live with my wife in Surrey, England, but occasionally we move around the country (most recently to Edinburgh, Scotland, during the pandemic) when the opportunity arises. My work allows me 45 days of working abroad per year (nine weeks), and then we have a generous annual leave policy on top of this. If you plan a bit and space things out, between this and my holidays I can spend a good chunk of any year travelling, and this is not including longer sabbaticals which are an option, too (that I will certainly execute!).

Harry's favourite thing about the 'digital nomad' life is ...

Honestly, I like being the master of each day. I can wake up and go to sleep when and where I like, as long as I deliver results for my team. I have found a company that trusts me to get on with it, and whether I log in at 9 a.m. or noon, from England, New Zealand, or a Greek Island, as long as I get the work done and make an impact, it doesn't matter where I am. Humans are hard-wired to roam, and most people suppress that these days, which is a shame, and against our evolutionary instinct.

Like most digital nomads, and most humans throughout time, I get itchy feet quickly, so looking at my calendar and seeing six trips planned brings me joy and relief in equal parts. You can't beat waking up to the sound of waves lapping on the Greek Island beach below your Airbnb, starting the day with a swim before walking along to the local taverna for a tentacle-fuelled lunch, running a couple of meetings with your feet in the sun and a Mythos beer hidden behind your laptop screen, and then finishing the day by logging off at 5 before driving to a secluded spot you've heard about on the other side of the small island you are on. This is possible, and in fact easy to do — if you set yourself up right!

His least favourite thing about the 'digital nomad' life is …

Bureaucracy — visas, tax implications, and remembering each country you've been to in the last ten years for some form. Absolute torture — why is this stuff not made easier? I will go and spend my money in the country that makes this the easiest!

The number one thing Harry wished he knew when he first started out as a digital nomad is …

Ditch the stereotypical image of what a 'digital nomad' is, and widen your view of what it can be. You don't need to be a freelancer, or have ten streams of micro-income, or run a blog, or be dirt poor, or give up your pension, or not have a normal 9 to 5. My 'style' of digital nomad living is to do both — have the 'standard' career but make it work for me and how I want to live my life.

Don't settle for a shit work environment that makes you come into the office three times a week. Challenge why you have to do anything like that. If you are good at what you do, it's a buyer's market when looking for jobs. There is no excuse these days for a company to worry too much about where you are physically located. COVID-19 is an absolute blessing in this sense — it shocked the world forward a decade in terms of working technology and acceptance and forced us to make remote working a thing. Don't accept that we have to go back from that. Leverage the shit out of it in your next job interview, or when looking for your next role. And there are also other ways of living the nomad life: regular sabbaticals. Work for six months, travel for six months. Or negotiate longer stretches of time off with your employer — two months here, two months there.

Never leave your job: ask for a one-year sabbatical. Best case, you have a job to come back to. Worst case, after one year you just decide not to come back and you are no worse off. Being a digital nomad is not necessarily just about working 'on the road'; in my (personal!) view; it's about doing whatever you can to maximize your time travelling, and only making the sacrifices that you want to make in order to have that happen. You can have both, but you have to ask or work to make it happen.

10

Working:

How to get the job done between flights, check-outs and adventures

~~~

In pretty much all the courses advertising the digital nomad life, you see a photo of an attractive young person sitting comfortably in shorts on a beach somewhere tropical, with their laptop open in front of them. Working from the beach is how the dream is sold, but it's generally a terrible idea. You get sand in your keyboard, sun reflecting off the screen, bad Wi-Fi and people splashing and jumping around everywhere. Plus, you can't enjoy the beach because, well, you're working! So, it's the worst of both worlds. You've ruined productivity and travel in one stroke. No thank you.

Working productively while embracing and enjoying strange foreign lands is a skill that you will need to develop to enjoy and succeed at the digital nomad life.

Choosing where you work

So if the beach is generally a terrible idea, what's better? It partly depends on what kind of work you are doing. For writing, I enjoy the energy and distraction of cafes and even bars. But for my standard business, which involves a lot of Zoom calls, I need somewhere quiet where I can focus without distraction or the risk of a dropped Wi-Fi connection. This is why I tend to get most of my heavy-duty work done from my accommodation. My Airbnb is typically my main office, and so this becomes an important factor to consider when booking a place to stay. Check the reviews and see if anyone mentions anything negative about the Wi-Fi connection. When booking your Airbnb accommodation, the host will list whether or not there is a 'laptop friendly workspace' in the features list. Other booking websites will have an equivalent, and checking out the photos can help.

If I can afford it, I like a place where there is a separate work space from the bedroom, although this isn't always possible, especially when travelling in more expensive places like western Europe or the United States. I find this helps a lot with anxiety, as I can 'leave work behind' when I go to bed, and also productivity, because it means you have a defined place to get things done. And if you travel in a couple, as I tend to, it can create much needed space and privacy.

Working from the Airbnb for the first few hours a day on business tasks and then moving in the afternoon to a cafe or bar for creative work like writing is my idea of a pretty good workday. When choosing cafes to work from, look out for places where others have their laptops out, but avoid places in the city centre and especially those with giant English menus outside that clearly cater to tourists. Finding a place with the right vibes, good internet connection, reasonable prices, strong coffee and maybe a good cocktail for later on is a challenge, and once I find one I tend to stick with it.

A cautionary tale about choosing your accommodation

If you have to spend a good part of your day on Zoom calls, you're probably going to end up doing a lot of your work at your accommodation. And this means where you stay is very important. Websites like Airbnb or Booking.com provide a layer of security and verification, so you know what you're booking and can read reviews from others (make sure to rely on written reviews, not just star ratings, and look out for recent reviews rather than ones two or three years old). I have in the past ventured past these websites and waded into the local rental markets. This will save you money, but may result in more adventure than you had bargained for …

A knock on the door

'Honey, did you hear that?'

It was a lazy Sunday evening and my partner Joanna and I were reading and scrolling on the couch in our apartment in Józsefváros, Budapest's infamous eighth district.

'No, hear what?' I replied.

'I thought I heard footsteps outside.'

Our apartment was in an orange-brick listed building that had once housed an artists' commune. The second floor, where we lived, housed myself and Joanna, and a demented old woman who screamed and shrieked and hurled objects whenever our voices were raised above the slightest whisper. One door led both to our apartment and hers, as well as a dusty balcony that overlooked the courtyard below. The woman shared her rooms with a semi-inanimate black cat and her degenerate, overweight son of 30-odd years.

'No one can access this part of the building, and anyway we locked the door,' I said.

The old lady went into manic fits of screaming whenever we forgot to lock the door to our shared part of the building. We were diligent about this when going out for the day, but if we left it unlocked while just ducking downstairs to pick up a delivery, she would step outside and start yelling. As a consequence, we never left the door unlocked for even a second. The old lady did not leave home except to yell at us, and that night we were quiet and well-behaved, and were not expecting company.

That's when I heard a knock on the door.

My heart accelerated. It was late, 9 or 10 p.m. on a weeknight. We were not playing loud music, talking loudly, or even breathing above a standard volume. We exchanged nervous glances. I went to the door.

The old woman's son stood there. Thin, blond hair. Fat. Dressed in ill-fitting clothes. 'Hello,' he said, in English.

'Um … hi,' I said. 'Eh … how can we help you?'

'It's this,' he said, pointing to his right leg, which I now noticed was in a blue plaster cast.

'They broke it,' the son continued, 'because I owe them money. If I don't pay them, they will break the other one …'

'Okay ... I'm so sorry,' I responded, with no idea of what else to say. The son spoke decent enough English, and we'd chatted once or twice on the old wooden staircase that led up from the dusty entrance hall to our shared part of the building, but we were by no means close.

'So,' he continued, 'I am very sorry, but I need to ask you to borrow me some money.'

I didn't answer.

'If I do not pay them,' he said again, 'they will do this to my other leg.' He gestured again at his cast.

'Um ...' I felt shocked, off balance, our quiet evening among the heaters and the couch and the books and Netflix unexpectedly interrupted.

'I need 5000 *forints*,' he said, naming an amount equivalent to about $15, 'or ...'

I got the message. I looked at Joanna, still on the couch, and she shrugged.

'Um, okay,' I said. I went to find my wallet, extracted a 5000-*forint* note, and handed it to him.

'Thank you,' he said. 'I promise, next week, I will pay you back.'

We stayed in that apartment for at least three more months, and we never saw him again.

Protecting your internet connection when working out of the home

These days you can find good Wi-Fi pretty much anywhere, but if you're venturing into more repressive countries, you may want to have a VPN (a virtual private network that disguises your internet traffic by sending your connection through overseas servers) installed so you can block firewalls. I use ExpressVPN but there are dozens of options and, despite what the advertisements say, not a huge difference between them. I have also found that setting your VPN to your home country can prevent online services from freaking out when they see you logging in from weird and wonderful IP addresses all over the world.

Creating temporary habits

Developing routines and finding regular places to work (even if for only a month or a couple of weeks) is a good way to increase productivity. You aren't getting much done if you're constantly moving cafes because the Wi-Fi is cutting out. This may require you to unlearn some of the travel habits that you may have formed during your past short-term trips. When you're passing through a place just for a few days, variety is king: you want to dine every night in a new restaurant, take your coffee every morning in a new cafe. But this is a huge drain of time and, most critically, energy. If your work is busy, then you want to know you can get it done.

This is why when I first settle into a place and plan to stay for a month or so, I begin by scouting things out. I'll set up a desk at the Airbnb for my laptop and webcam. I'll determine a couple of decent cafes where I can get work done. I'll make sure the apartment is well stocked with coffee, and even buy a cheap plunger if need be (because life is far too short for instant coffee).

Making the most of uncertainty

Sometimes even the best plans don't work out. Your Airbnb internet crashes. The water isn't running at your favourite cafe. A beggar is tapping you on the shoulder as you try to write. Your bank has blocked your credit card because it thought you were robbing yourself from strange countries. You can't remember that email password. These things can be much more stressful to deal with on the road without the stability and infrastructure that you usually rely on. Also, everything is in a foreign language, the currency is incomprehensible, and the local time zone is bamboozling and making you perform algebra gymnastics every time you schedule a Zoom call.

But then you pack up your laptop and look around for a few minutes. You see people dressed in strange attire. Exotic writing on every sign. Maybe you have started to understand a few words of the local language, perhaps even enough to order your next coffee and beer like a local. You are recognized at the small hole-in-the-wall eatery, and feel comfortable enough to slightly zone out as you wander the streets. You are purposeful, but also aimless. You are far from home, yet also ensconced in familiar habits. You are experiencing adventure, and the creativity and motivation starts to come back.

You will simply not have as much control over your environment as you would at home. Control the things you can and plan out your day as much as possible, but also learn to see this chaos and uncertainty as a source of energy and inspiration. It isn't going away, so you may as well learn to make the most of it.

Use the right state of mind for the right job

The logistics of travel, especially when pandemic restrictions are a thing (they aren't really now as I write this in mid-2022, but will they be when this is published in 2023? Who knows!) do your head in. Flights, visas, airport transfers, accommodation bookings, SIM cards and roaming rates all require a certain kind of energy and focus. I use times when I am not feeling particularly creative to handle stuff like my bookkeeping, admin and all the tedium that comes from moving and existing and getting things done in the modern world.

And when I do feel creative, I embrace that too. I make plans for new products or businesses, write articles or chapters, reach out to people to network and form connections. Recognizing what kind of work matches your own mood and frame of mind best is a potent productivity hack for when travelling and navigating uncertainty.

Learning how to switch off

'Are you sure it's safe?' Joanna asked. Or maybe I asked her. Whichever one of us replied 'Yes' must have been convincing enough, because the ancient, creaking, clanking Ferris wheel was soon bearing us high above the hills overlooking Tbilisi, in Georgia.

'Can you see our apartment?' I asked, looking down below the green hills and then left along the Mtkvari River towards a modern, densely built-up area of the city known as Subartalo. My phone vibrated. I took it out and saw there was an email notification from a client asking for an update on a project. Immediately, my mind was hijacked. I fired off an email in response, put my phone back in my pocket, looked out the window for the view and …

'That was quick,' Joanna said, as the door opened and we hopped out onto firm ground. Although I had been on the Ferris wheel, I'd missed the ride.

Long-term travel means relearning how your mind works. It's about discovering new and different ways to be productive. It's about knowing when you create, when you organize, and when you need to switch off and enjoy the moment. Below are some strategies for switching off that have worked for me.

» Turn off notifications. When that phone vibrates, it hijacks your mind. I am very selective when work notifications (email, Slack, Microsoft Teams, whatever your clients or employers impose on you) are enabled and when they are not. My emails are still there, but no notifications mean I choose when to focus on them, rather than allowing them to claim my focus whenever something comes up.

» Do what you need to do, then stop. I am the kind of person who relaxes best after the work is done. This sounds like a truism, but 'after the work is done' is the ambiguous part of that sentence. Like most creatives, there is of course an unlimited amount of work to do. That's why I break down big tasks, like writing a book, into smaller chunks. When the chunk you have assigned yourself for the day is done, stop, close your laptop, and go and explore the city you're in.

» Set boundaries with clients and employers. Make sure clients know when you are reachable and when you are not. Clients will contact you outside of these hours anyway, but you do not need to respond (and indeed you shouldn't) because it's not what you signed up for and agreed upon. The first few times you ignore that work email that falls outside hours will be stressful, but then you'll realize that the sky didn't fall, and it will gradually get easier and easier.

As you learn how to mitigate uncertainties on the road, controlling your circumstances where possible and channelling uncertainty into creativity when it's not possible, you will find that you can be just as productive and efficient as a digital nomad as you would be at home. Just maybe not at the beach!

MEET THE NOMADS

Name: Bart Och

Polish/British nationality, mid-thirties, based in the UK.

Mostly travels: With his long-term partner/spouse.

Currently in: Rome, Italy.

Digital nomad experience: Four or more years.

Has lived/worked/travelled in: France, Italy, Netherlands, Poland, Spain, Switzerland, Cambodia, Hong Kong, Indonesia, Laos, Malaysia, Singapore and Vietnam.

Normally stays in a country/city for: A month or so.

Makes a living as a: Freelance photographer and writer.

Meet Bart

I am a photographer and writer. I am also the founder of *DEFUZE* magazine at DEFUZEmag.co.uk. I have also recently started my personal blog at lovagabondo.com. I often work with hotels, tour agencies and even modelling agencies (I used to be a fashion photographer) to support my nomadic lifestyle. During the pandemic, I taught English in Vietnam where I worked and lived for two years.

How Bart got started

I grew up in Poland, but since I can remember I have always wanted to travel the world. But all I was ever told was to enjoy my childhood years because life only gets worse after one graduates — you get a job, a mortgage, settle down and let time fly by. I think it was my biggest fear at the time and I have always resented the idea of predetermined life. After one year at university, I dropped out and moved to London. Working menial jobs to get by, I developed a hobby: photography. This, plus my new British passport, were to become my tickets out of the predetermined life.

As soon as I had my new passport in hand, I booked a one-way flight to India. I did a bit of couchsurfing there in Mumbai and Goa. I loved it — the chaos, the smells, the noise ... Then I went to Sri Lanka and so on. It all happened back in 2017, and I didn't think this life I chose for myself on a whim was going to continue to this day. I don't have a home and so I pay no rent and no bills. I don't have a car or any contracts. This may be strange and scary to some because we are taught to always prepare for the future. I choose to live for the now, in the present moment. I don't worry too much about what will happen tomorrow and just deal with things as they come. I also taught myself photography and marketing and acquired a bunch of certificates, such as TEFL, which I can use to teach English as a foreign language.

While I was living in London and was into fashion photography, I also started a fashion magazine at DEFUZEmag.co.uk, which is not something huge, but it does generate enough traction for me to be able to do what I do. It is a lot of work because I started this whole thing on my own having learned a lot about digital publishing. Now, my partner mostly takes care of it. I also dabble in writing and I hope to establish myself as a professional writer one day. Until then, we just pick up small gigs here and there, whether it is teaching English, photography or writing, marketing or product reviews.

Honestly, I don't really enjoy a job that ties me into a contract or a 9 to 5 routine. In Asia, it is easy to save up and so having worked there for a while, we saved up a bunch of money and then we didn't have to worry about working for a while after we left.

Bart's 'typical day'

When I am not discovering new caves (semi-joking), I often do a bit of work in the morning writing or editing photos, then I have breakfast and see what is there to do that I haven't done yet — not necessarily in that order (I once had breakfast for lunch). In all seriousness, I like to travel on a budget. Because I studied journalism and have a magazine, a lot of tourist attractions I normally would have to pay for are free for me. I am flexible in terms of my travels, too, so I pick days on which flights are cheap when I feel it is time to move. I don't buy souvenirs or dine in lavish restaurants and tend to cook at 'home', and by home I mean an apartment.

We tend to stay at least a month in one place and rent our accommodation, which is much more affordable than staying in a hotel or Airbnb. On occasion, we stay in hostels or hotels if they would like us to write about them, do some photography and marketing. Often it happens that we jump between five-star hotels and ramshackle hostels, small city apartments, mountains or beach cabins and big homes. I stopped having expectations about where I stay so I am pretty happy with anything as long as I have a bed, water and some food. I am no stranger to sleeping on the floor, on a beach or on a street; I appreciate simply having a roof over my head.

In Asia, it is much cheaper, of course, so I have no problem booking a place for a few nights, somewhere cosy, maybe a homestay with a local family or someplace near the beach. In India, I stayed in a homestay where I had a free bed in return for a little bit of charity work (sweeping the floor, tending to animals or helping out in the kitchen). We also stayed in an off-grid cabin in the middle of the jungle in Borneo during the wet season to basically take care of a dog and to make sure no local trekkers who happened to stumble upon the place broke in or stole anything.

Bart's favourite thing about the 'digital nomad' life is ...

Freedom, versatility and excitement. I can pack my bag at a drop of a dime and move from place to place as I please. I rarely get bored, 'stuck' or 'used to' things and places.

His least favourite thing about the 'digital nomad' life is ...

Having to say 'goodbye' more than anyone should ever have to do to people that I may never see again. Also, overcoming cultural and language barriers.

The number one thing Bart wished he knew when he first started out as a digital nomad is ...

That it isn't just some glorified hobby. Anyone can do it if they are willing to live life differently to most people.

11

Borders:

Staying legal when living in the grey area

~~~

The authorities who govern our world and guard nations' borders like to fit people into neat boxes. But what of the digital nomad, who belongs everywhere and nowhere? It's hard to take a man seriously when he's standing underneath two portraits of a blond, overweight reality TV star. And yet I tried to ignore the images of the US president and pay attention to US border guard Agent Shane. He had a gun. He had my passport. And he was not smiling. 'Sir, can you tell me why you were in Iran?'

'I was there with friends as part of a charity drive. It's called the Mongol Rally, basically we drove from Europe to—'

'Were you there alone?'

'No sir, I was in a group of eight friends from New Zealand, as part of a charity event called the—'

'And why are you here?'

'To attend a marketing conference on behalf of a company.'

'What is your role in the company?'

'Um ...' I hesitated while trying to think on my feet, 'marketing director.'

That final exaggeration seemed to make a difference. The officer's manner changed and I was invited to take a seat. Around me sat about half a dozen other travellers in assorted states of dishevelment. A Hispanic grandmother in a wheelchair and her two grandsons, both dressed in hoodies, tattooed, sullen, arms folded. A tall Taiwanese man dressed in a fashionable jacket and Nike shoes. Two thuggish bald men sitting next to each other, their bellies bursting out of their stained T-shirts.

The room was white, brightly lit, and situated downstairs below the main immigration queue. Four uniformed officers — mostly bald, bearded and pale — strode in and out with purpose. They gossiped with each other and seemed constantly in search of lost forms. 'Did you see the D366?' 'Steve has it.' 'Print another one.' 'The computer won't print.' 'Did you login as "staff"?'

Behind our room was an interrogation cell, where a man whom I couldn't see was getting his luggage thoroughly searched. Two officers were chatting about the Taiwanese man: 'Did he buy a flight back home?'

'No, he spoke to his travel agent.'

'Well, tell him if he doesn't buy one now and get on a flight this evening he's going to detention.'

One of the agents turned to the Taiwanese man who stood nervously in the corner hunched over his suitcase. 'Hey buddy!'

The Taiwanese man looked up.

'Buddy, you didn't buy that flight. You missed out. The only other one is $13,000. Economy is sold out.'

The man shrugged and took out his phone. He placed a call and began speaking in Mandarin, translating the offer to someone on the other end.

Turning to his colleagues, the officer said, 'He coulda had that other flight for like 500 bucks, but he didn't do it and now he's gotta pay $13,000!'

Turning back to the Taiwanese man he exclaimed, 'Hey buddy, now you gotta pay $13,000!'

One of the young Hispanic men was called up. He walked with an aggressive roll of the shoulders, and leered pugnaciously at the officer.

'You from Colombia?'

'Yes.'

'First time in the US?'

'No.'

'You here to work illegally?'

'No.'

'Got family here?'

'Yes.'

'Do you have any criminal convictions?'

'No.'

'It's not what it says here, buddy.'

He was led off to the back room.

Other unfortunates came and went. Men from Norway, women from Russia, children — unaccompanied — from China. Some were eventually handed documents and allowed to leave. Others were sent to detention. The agents kept score: 'That's thirteen in detention today already!'

The Colombian grandmother sat still in her wheelchair as each of her grandsons faced interrogation in turn. Occasionally, one of the officers spoke to her in Spanish. Within her hearing, they gossiped in English about the two young men. After the second young man had been away for about an hour, an agent said, 'Okay, I want her to see her grandkids getting deported.'

Now they were talking about me, referring to me as 'Iran.' 'Shane, you working on Iran?'

'Yeah.'

'It's a TTPA.'

'Yeah.'

'You did a TTPA yesterday, let me handle this one.'

'Okay, you sure?'

'Yeah.'

The new agent called me up. They'd apparently decided I was no threat, and his approach was warmer than his colleague's. 'Sir, can you tell me why you went to Iran?'

'I went there as part of a charity event called the Mongol Rally. It's a drive from Europe to Mongolia through Central Asia, to raise money for a charity.'

'Oh! Like that TV show! What's it called …'

'Um … *The Amazing Race*?'

'No! Hey, what's it called? That show? It's like that show you have on the TV …'

'I'm not sure, sir.'

'*Top Gear*! That's right. It's just like *Top Gear*.'

It was nothing like *Top Gear*. 'Absolutely.'

'You here for business?'

'Yes, to attend a marketing conference in Salem.'

'In Salem?'

'Yes.'

'I'm from Salem! Oh, you're gonna love it there, sir!'

At this point the agent's manner went from warm to almost deferential, as he explained the situation to me. 'Okay, sir. So because you were in Iran, your ESTA is no longer valid. What we're going to do is issue you a visa so you can come to the States and do your conference. But before you come back again, you're gonna have to go to the US embassy in New Zealand and apply for another visa. You cannot return to the United States before you do that.'

'Thank you, I understand.'

'It's a new law, sir. You haven't done anything wrong, and we're gonna get you sorted out. It shouldn't take too long. Do you have someone waiting to pick you up?'

'The company is sending a driver.'

'Okay, so you wanna call them and let them know you'll be about an hour longer. We'll be as quick as possible.'

'I will, thank you.'

As I took out my phone to call the driver, another agent shouted at a Hispanic man sitting in the back of the room. 'Oi, no phones! Can't you see the sign? The sign right there! Put your goddam phone away!' Guiltily, I placed my call and sat back down.

The next hour passed slowly. More people came and went. A young man with a few drink-driving convictions, sent here by immigration staff who smelled alcohol on his breath. A middle-aged man whose dual citizenship had baffled officials. A pale-faced man from Kazakhstan, who sat nervously clutching his aqua-blue passport, rocking back and forth in his seat. Some were let through. Some were sent to detention. Some booked flights over the phone, and returned home.

My agent now held my passport in his hand. He asked for a signature, and was about to let me go when his computer started causing problems. Before this, they'd had to find their boss to validate my temporary visa. But they didn't know where he was. He had since been located and my documents were now in order, giving me just under a month in the USA. They'd even waived the $585 fee, as indicated on the forms. I was relieved, and ready to go. But the computer was not cooperating. 'It won't save the event!' 'Did you change the status before you created the event?' 'John did.' 'I thought Steve was working on it?' 'Steve's eating.'

This went on for some time, until finally the computer cooperated and I was free to go. Three hours had gone by. It felt like much longer. Many of the same faces who'd been there when I arrived still sat, silent and sullen, on the brown couches.

Border fear

Perhaps this experience I have just described is why I still get anxious every time I need to cross a border. Or maybe it's just in my nature: different people get anxious about different things. Apparently, Sigmund Freud would show up at train stations three hours ahead of time, so anxious was he to not miss a train. Maybe I have something of that bug too. Hours, probably cumulative days, spent at airports and border crossings across the world has yet to dent the fear.

I still remember being taken downstairs at the American airport after they found the Iranian stamp in my passport. I remember the Kyrgyzstani and Turkmen border guards, swaggering in sunglasses, bragging about how much they were ripping us off for bribes. Every trip, I still sweat the documentation. I am a conscientious person: when I write, I hit my deadlines. I want to do things by the book. But with my lifestyle, it's not always possible to be 100 per cent pure. There are grey areas, and as a digital nomad those are often where you will live. As a holder of a British passport who spends much of my time in Europe, Brexit has amplified these anxieties. It's been quite an experience to have freedom of movement across this fascinating and diverse continent, only to lose it in one fell swoop. The bureaucracy in the wake of Brexit has been the source of a lot of anxiety. And to be honest, I am still figuring it out.

The internet can be a wonderful source of utter nonsense on this topic. Fear-mongering posts can make you so scared of accidentally violating a visa rule that you never want to leave your house again. At the same time, you look at the lifestyles of people who travel long-term, and you wonder how on earth they do it, all the while working and presumably banking the money somewhere (see Chapter 9).

My own approach has been a mixture of anxious planning and improvisation. Laws change and those that are actually enforced don't always match up with what you will read on government websites and the like. When planning how long you can get away with staying in a certain place, it can help to look at the actual, real experience of others with a similar passport at a given time.

For example, if you are a New Zealand citizen wondering if you can spend more than three months in Europe, official government websites may say no. But a little research will uncover bloggers like Bren on the Road (https://brenontheroad.com/new-zealand-bilateral-visa-waivers-schengen/) who explains that, because of historic visa waiver agreements New Zealand made with various European countries, it's actually possible to 'overstay' in many countries without consequence, provided you follow the specific terms of each agreement. The comments section bears this out, with Kiwis and others attesting to their own experience.

If you google terms like 'Canadian citizen border crossing in Spain' (substituting your own country of origin with your choice of border crossing), you can read about the experience of real travellers and what they have actually faced. Then you can make your own decisions based on this information, while staying within the laws as best you can.

Being a nomad often means finding yourself falling into ill-defined legal grey areas. And, normally, I take the risk. We're figuring this out as we go, and so are the powers that be. Arm yourself with as much knowledge as possible about the on-the-ground realities, educate yourself about any exceptions or loopholes that apply, and make informed decisions about the risks. This can be stressful and sometimes I do yearn for the comfort and security of a black-and-white existence. But then, I remind myself why I am doing this, and imagine what lies on the other side of that flight.

MEET THE NOMADS

Name: Henry Worsley

Age nineteen, from the UK.

Mostly travels: Alone.

Currently in: Oxford, England.

Digital nomad experience: One year.

Has lived/worked/travelled in: Egypt, Iraq, Jordan, Kyrgyzstan and Ukraine.

Normally stays in a country/city for: A month or so.

Makes a living as a: Freelancer (writer/journalist), tour-guide, builder, shepherd.

Meet Henry

I'm a student, freelance journalist and travel guide. I'm currently writing predominantly on Ukraine (where I lived for two months last year) for online magazines and newspapers such as *REACTION* and *The Scotsman*. Last year, I balanced my work with an eight-month trip from Alexandria to China in the footsteps of Marco Polo.

How Henry got started

For almost all of last year I was something you could really call 'nomadic'. I moved from place to place, following the path of the ancient Silk Road from Alexandria to the Chinese border. I did everything on a shoestring. I earned money from odd jobs; an example would be my work in Kyrgyzstan. When I arrived in the capital, Bishkek, I was put in touch with a friend of a friend; she had lived in Italy for years (meaning we had a language in common), and had decided to open Kyrgyzstan's first proper pizzeria. It wasn't a success — she told me that five hungry Kyrgyz farmers would often order one pizza between them, growing furious when they realized it wasn't enough. Anyway, this pizzaiola found me a job as a shepherd, which included free food and accommodation for as long as I wanted. The only caveat was that most of my day would be made up of hard labour, shovelling dung in the thin air of the Tian Shan mountains. I spent a few weeks up there, but in the end the isolation, the heat, the yak castration — it got to me. I had to move on.

That's an example of the sort of job I did, jobs that were found thanks to friends of friends of friends. And I saved more money on accommodation by almost exclusively staying with locals via the Couchsurfing website. In all honesty, I can't really pinpoint how I settled into a nomadic lifestyle; I had booked a one-way ticket to Cairo and I just went wherever it felt natural to go.

Henry's 'typical day'

A typical day (at the moment) would mean waking up to the bells of Oxford, scouring the book shelves of the old Bodleian library, preparing an essay for a tutorial or an exam. A few months ago there were no bells. In March 2022 I was writing from Transnistria (a disputed territory on the Moldavan/Ukrainian border) where I would wake up (often with a terrible hangover from my host's homemade vodka), then interview Ukrainian refugees or local dissidents. My host Victor would hurriedly cook me up some *grechka* in his pokey Soviet-built flat, and then it was back to work, talking to as many people as possible, rapidly writing up articles for anyone in the UK willing to print them.

Describing a typical day is difficult, because I really try to avoid any kind of strict, self-improvement-esque routine, the kind of thing Matt D'Avella [a Netflix filmmaker and social media influencer who speaks on productivity] would want to see me doing. I read somewhere that routine is the death of most people because it can make time pass so quickly. A lack of concrete structure makes my life random, scattered, perhaps a little stressful, but I feel like I appreciate everything a bit more because of it.

Henry's favourite thing about the 'digital nomad' life is ...

The lyrics of 'Free Bird' by Lynyrd Skynyrd (glorious guitar solo!) describe it best.

**His least favourite thing about
the 'digital nomad' life is …**

Missing Mum's cooking.

**The number one thing Henry wished he knew
when he first started out as a digital nomad is …**

You don't get lonely. There are always characters you'll meet
on the road, you just have to be open.

~~~~~~~~~~~~~~~~~~~~~~~~~~~~~~~~~~~~~~

12

Stillness:
Sometimes, it's
okay to slow down

~~

At first, travel is its own reason. It is life, work, adventure and creativity all rolled into one. It's a break from the ordinary, and every moment is exciting. And then ... it begins to wear on you. The excitement of a place is often inversely correlated with comfort. This makes sense. To be challenged is to be captivated. When every day is diverting, fascinating and perhaps uncomfortable, then the immediate experience of being alive is riveting. A trip to the supermarket yields enough stories for three dinner parties. But, of course, this often isn't good for getting work done.

Small irritations begin to pile up. The isolation of not being able to communicate fully in the native language anywhere you go. The frustration of dodgy internet connections. The yearning for a clean set of clothes. And so you get to a point where you long to slow the pace. You extend your stay from one month to two ... to three ... to six. Maybe even a year. Your surroundings are no longer novel, and you are no longer a stranger. Yes, there's still a lot more to learn, and you're certainly far from having solved the mystery of the foreign land in which you've ended up. But when does a digital nomad simply become ... an expat?

In 2021, my wife and I lived in Tbilisi, Georgia. We moved there from Spain, bringing with us literally everything we owned in two bulging suitcases. (I maintain, for the record, that her shoes took up the bulk of at least one of them.) We then followed what has become something of a formula for arriving in an unfamiliar country and possible home base for the first time.

Shortly before leaving Spain, we booked a hotel for our first few days, and took them up on their offer of an airport transfer. As we'd be arriving in Tbilisi at the dead of night, laden with all our earthly possessions, we wanted to avoid the hassle of haggling for a cab or figuring out a bus system. On the first day, we worked in the morning, before setting out to wander: walking without much aim across the city, exploring the winding streets of the old town, the roaring roads by the sleepy river, the parks with their stray dogs and churches.

After acquiring a bit of a feel for the layout of the city, we went on Airbnb and found a place for our first month. It was in Surbatalo, a modern part of the city, on the eighteenth floor of a high rise. Initial impressions upon arrival were a bit scary: the door to the building was broken, the handle long since removed, and it banged shut with a horrible metallic thump every time someone charged through. The elevator rattled and shook horribly between floors, and the Russian woman standing beside us in our first ride in it smoked a cigarette and stubbed it out under her high-heeled shoe when her floor arrived.

The apartment itself was nice and the views took in the Georgian hills in the north towards the Russian border and the not-so-Georgian chains of Holiday Inn, McDonald's and Wednesdays which occupied the centre and edges of the packed highway below us. It was during a COVID-19 resurgence in mid 2021, and I sat on the balcony in the evenings and watched the river of traffic slow to a trickle as the 9 p.m. curfew approached, until I could see nothing but the blue lights of police cars patrolling for stragglers.

Towards the end of the month, we re-evaluated our situation. We could do what we had done in Spain, and make a private deal with the apartment host for a longer rental. We could move to another city, or we could stay in Tbilisi but move apartments. Liking Tbilisi but yearning for a more traditional and less 'concrete jungle' feel, we checked out and schlepped our bags halfway across the city to an Airbnb in Avlabari. It was here that we arrived on the day of a death in the building, and witnessed chain-smoking mourners gather throughout the evening until the strictly enforced curfew sent them away. Avlabari was a world of crumbling buildings, stray dogs, historic Armenian churches and small bakeries where you could get an oval slab of Georgian bread for loose change. The apartment was comfortable and the neighbourhood raw and captivating (dare one say 'authentic'), but the slow Wi-Fi at the Airbnb made work tricky. Struggling through video conferences late into the night with a new client whom one needs to impress is not ideal, so we decided to move once again.

At this point, facing our third move of literally all our possessions in as many months, the process was getting a bit tiresome. The wrestle with the overflowing suitcases. The daily war to find clean socks. The scramble to polish the Airbnb and return it to an unlived-in state, lest a bad review make it harder to find our next home. Moving was a two-day, full-time job. We did this for another two or so months, with one more Airbnb sitting above a waterfall right in the heart of Tbilisi's old town. In the evening we heard the frogs cackling away, and our apartment was decorated floor to ceiling with traditional Georgian paintings, ram's horn goblets and Orthodox religious symbols.

The excitement was there, always, but the angst and frustration and exhaustion of moving everything so often was starting to become a dominant theme. It was time to make a change. To slow down. To lean in, at least temporarily, to stability. To allow my wife to acquire more shoes. And so we moved for a while back to Poland, acquired a storage unit for excess clothes, and focused for some months on business and family and reconnecting with a local community.

Being a 'digital nomad' is about freedom, but the lifestyle itself can sometimes feel like a trap: the obligations encircle you, until you find yourself spending more time packing and unpacking and stressing about Wi-Fi connections and daily obstacles than you do either enjoying and appreciating where you are or getting useful things done. And when that happens, it's okay to take yourself off the field for a while. To actually unpack. To recharge, refocus, refuel psychologically and financially, and figure out where you want to be next.

If you are experiencing traveller's burnout, here are a few tips that could help.

Remember your why

For me, it's wandering about on strange streets, getting lost, and watching the sun set on an unfamiliar town, knowing that tomorrow brings more possibilities for adventure and discovery. What is it all for? Make a conscious effort to reconnect with this. Remember those times when you felt most alive and excited while travelling. The ingredients that make up that feeling are still out there. Sometimes, when travel becomes routine and the routine becomes a chore, it can help you to remember what it was that sent you out your door in the first place.

Mix things up

If you're sick of Airbnbs, stay for a few days in a nice hotel to recharge. Or look up a local friend and crash on their couch. Or track down a campsite in the country you find yourself in, get hold of a tent, and reconnect. Break the routine and travel in a new way. A long train journey if you're sick of flying. Renting a car and driving if you're sick of trains. Walking to another side of the city. Mix up your 'how' and you can jolt yourself back into a new groove of excitement and adventure.

Recharge yourself creatively

Having a book that I'm working on outside of my day-to-day commercial projects has been a huge comfort, sense of stability and creative renewal during my travels. Some find this through journalling, blogging, painting, photography or writing old-fashioned letters home. Over time, your body of work builds up, and you document something tangible from your travels.

Remember how far you've come

And not just geographically. I remember in my early solo-wanderings when I was seventeen and eighteen, I was scared half to death half the time. Foreign train travel was a constant terror of missing a stop. I remember pacing for an hour outside a bakery in France trying to muster the courage to put my high-school French to the test and order a *croque-monsieur*. Now, when you are so confident in your travels that riding a train across a border somewhere can seem boring, it helps to remember that it was once a huge challenge.

Travel somewhere more challenging

If the exciting and mysterious streets of Europe are now as familiar to you as your hometown, then it might be time to raise the stakes and challenge yourself. Travelling and working around India for three weeks was, for me, a chance to reconnect with travel as an encompassing, overwhelming experience, where the knowledge of being somewhere new and exotic occupies every inch of your consciousness. And doing this while trying to work and run my business was a whole different kind of challenge, one I am grateful for and which made me appreciate the relative familiarity of Europe that much more upon my return.

Take a break

Being a digital nomad means travel is always an option, but it's never an obligation. It's fine to extend that Airbnb booking by a few months. It's fine to return home, unpack and gorge yourself on your mother's cooking. It's fine to establish a base somewhere and use that as a launching pad for short-term travel. You don't constantly have to be notching up new stamps in your passport. It's okay to slow down.

~~~~~~

MEET THE NOMADS

Name: Justin Dynia

Young working professional, early twenties, from the United States.

Mostly travels: Alone.

Currently in: Boston.

Digital nomad experience: Less than one year.

Has lived/worked/travelled in: Spain, France and Portugal.

Normally stays in a country/city for: Less than one month.

Makes a living as a: Political communications specialist.

Meet Justin

I currently serve as the Communications Director for Representative Kevin G. Honan in the Massachusetts House of Representatives. My daily duties include managing media relations, social media and website content, and assisting with policy work and constituent services. Most of my work can be conducted remotely from any time zone. I'm a writer by training and worked as a reporter and editor for the majority of my time in university. Language is also a part of my daily work, as I am fluent in English, Spanish and Portuguese, so I can connect with different communities. My skills and experience in politics, journalism and language give me a comprehensive blend of writing and field work which is why I mostly label myself as a communications expert.

How Justin got started

I had the pleasure of studying and working abroad in Madrid for two months in 2020. However, I had the displeasure of evacuating the country during the onset of the pandemic. It remained my dream to return to Europe, and I fulfilled that dream after my graduation from Boston University in May 2022. After a week in Madrid and Seville with my parents, I set off solo for eleven days in France and Portugal. My passions for travelling and writing have always existed, but I only began to blend them on this trip. I created and designed my own website and worked on two projects I felt were unique and encapsulated my experiences. More than just learning to love myself and the world around me, travel writing has shown me the power of inspiring others to fulfil their own travel journeys in whatever forms they may come.

Justin's 'typical day'

No two days are clone copies, but an average day for me begins when I leave my hostel by 10 a.m. latest with my laptop, journal, a book, and all the other intangibles. Most mornings I spend at cafes journalling, writing and reading. Only once I have my espresso and some food do I go about my day, which involves getting lost in museums, shopping, chatting with locals, eating and drinking heartily, and a gruelling amount of walking and sightseeing. I take notes throughout the day and do some writing in my hostel before a quick shower and heading to dinner, sometimes with new friends and sometimes with a book to keep me company. At night I conduct most of my interviews, because restaurants serve lots of 'Honesty Juice' to locals who are more than happy to talk to a nice foreigner asking them intimate questions such as 'Where do you find love in your life?' By the time my head finally hits the pillow, I am satisfied by the exhausting but fulfilling day behind me and already excited for the meaningful day ahead.

Justin's favourite thing about the 'digital nomad' life is ...

The freedom of exploring my passions in foreign places and connecting with other communities in their native language.

His least favourite thing about the 'digital nomad' life is ...

Sore shoulders from hauling around a few weeks' worth of belongings in a duffel bag and a backpack.

The number one thing Justin wished he knew when he first started out as a digital nomad is ...

Strangers are always much more open and willing to share information with you than one would think.

13

Places:

Advice on choosing where to go, based on what YOU want

~~~

The people interviewed for this book have lived, worked and travelled as digital nomads in:

Afghanistan	Mexico	Hong Kong	St Martin
Argentina	Nepal	Iceland	Sweden
Australia	New Zealand	India	Switzerland
Austria	Denmark	Indonesia	Tajikistan
Brazil	Dominica	Iraq	Thailand

Bulgaria	Ecuador	Ireland	The Bahamas
Cambodia	Egypt	Italy	The Netherlands
Chile	El Salvador	Jamaica	Trinidad & Tobago
China	England	Jordan	Turkey
Colombia	Estonia	Panama	UK
Costa Rica	Fiji	Peru	Ukraine
Croatia	France	Poland	USA
Kyrgyzstan	Germany	Portugal	Uzbekistan
Laos	Ghana	Russia	Vietnam
Malaysia	Greece	Singapore	
Malta	Grenada	Spain	

I would add to this list Albania and Georgia. One thing many (though not all) of these countries have in common is that, compared to Western Europe, Australia, New Zealand or North America, the cost of living is very cheap. This means that if you earn in pounds or dollars but spend in *zloty* or in *forint*, you can live relatively well for considerably less. This is what some call 'geo-arbitrage' and it's a big word for a simple but important idea.

The old idea of a 'vacation' saw travel as a costly departure from life, something to be saved up for. Backpacking, while cheaper, is also something that comes between or before work, forcing you to live on the cheap in hostels, environments that are incredible for socializing but not particularly conducive to productivity. 'Nomading' is different. If you're working several hours a day, you need a bit more comfort. But you're probably staying for a month or two, not just a few days like you would on a vacation. Because this isn't a big, rare event to save up for — it's your everyday life — you need to budget accordingly.

Because of this, living in relatively cheap places with relatively weak currencies like Eastern Europe or South-East Asia is a popular and logical choice for nomads. But that doesn't mean you have to confine yourself to these parts of the world. Internet connectivity is more prevalent than you may think, and plenty of nomads manage to earn enough on the road to enjoy middle-class style living, even in expensive places like New Zealand or Scandinavia. With remote work this is more and more accessible, especially if you don't mind the odd early morning or late night to compensate for time zones. Where you live and travel as a nomad, then, lies somewhere in the matrix of means, priorities and personal taste.

Optimizing for affordability

Places that are affordable are often so because there's more supply — in terms of accommodation and infrastructure — than demand. They will also probably have a weak currency (i.e. not the Euro) and a fairly low average wage, meaning it's hard for the locals to travel abroad. Be sensitive to this if you choose to take advantage of the financial power geo-arbitrage may give you, and spend your money judiciously at locally owned establishments so that your presence there is a benefit and a plus to the local economy.

If cheapness is what you desire, then Georgia is a classic choice. A meal out in a nice restaurant with plenty of local wine can run to the equivalent of just five or six Australian dollars. Apartment prices are often exploitative, however, as local landlords catch on to the digital nomad boom. Tapping local expat networks (as explained in Chapter 4) may help shortcut this process.

Other small countries outside the European Union but still on the fringes of Europe, like Albania, Armenia and Serbia, are also great spots. You'll find unlimited adventure at very affordable prices, with tolerable infrastructure. While technically in the European Union and the Eurozone, Bulgaria also ticks these boxes. Flitting between Europe's single-visa Schengen Zone (the shared border area which links together most European Union countries and some others like Norway and Switzerland into one giant shared region for travellers, meaning you can travel all the way from Poland to Portugal without a single passport check) and other adjacent countries like those described above can also be a good way for Brits, Americans and Kiwis/Aussies to maximize their visa allowance in Europe.

Optimizing for efficiency

I've mentioned before the trade-off most digital nomads must face at some stage between adventure and productivity. While you will eventually get in the habit of being able to be efficient from anywhere, sometimes you need to be in a place where things work, you can more easily communicate, and hey (no shame) there's maybe a gosh-darned Starbucks. I've personally found the Costa Brava in Spain, specifically Torrevieja, a good choice here. I ended up there quite accidentally during one of the COVID-19 lockdowns and was happily stranded for a few months. It's utterly pleasant and completely unexciting, and the rent is surprisingly affordable, cheaper even than I found in Georgia. (The best deal I have encountered is 400 Euro/month for a nice apartment in Torrevieja, compared to 600ish in Tbilisi, and just 200 in Sarande, Albania.)

The idea here is to look for small-ish off-season towns in developed countries, such as Sziget in Hungary outside of festival season, or Sicily or Sardinia in November. You get the infrastructure you need to be able to enjoy working in a pleasant location, without the rip-off bustle of hyper tourism. This kind of getaway is perfect if you need a month or two to recharge the batteries.

Optimizing for adventure

While I still believe Europe has basically unlimited potential for adventure, particularly in the East and in the Balkans, much of the bolder digital 'nomading' takes place in South-East Asia. Countries like Thailand actively court digital nomads with visa options and attractive tax rates, and cities like Chiang Mai are virtual nomad meccas. This may be tiresome for some if your idea of an adventure is not to sit in a Thai cafe sipping a latte surrounded by Canadians on MacBooks, but bases like this are great starting points for real exploration.

Once you're embedded in a region like this, it's easy to travel on weekend trips to surrounding countries, to rent a bike and get out of the city, to learn a little of the local language and get far from the tourist bubble. (I speak about how to do this kind of thing in more depth in my book *Travel Your Way: Rediscover the world on your own terms*).

Optimizing for networking

I've written before about how I've made some of the most valuable business relationships while travelling. Many of the relationships with people I still work with and consider both friends and colleagues were formed when I lived in China around 2015 and 2016. At that time China was much more open to foreigners than it is now at the time of writing, and plenty of young folks there were searching for something between adventure and opportunity. In 2022, China is a much more difficult place to get established, so you may ask yourself 'Where is next?' Perhaps it's East Africa or Vietnam or Latin America. Somewhere where exciting things are happening and careers are being made, and interesting people are being drawn to the electric charge. We're still coming out of the 2020 pandemic at the time of writing, and the footfalls have yet to make themselves loudly heard. But listen closely.

~~~~~~

MEET THE NOMADS

Name: Ivy Raff

From Queens, New York, with Eastern European immigrant heritage, late thirties.

Mostly travels: With her long-term partner/spouse.

Currently in: Detroit, Michigan, US.

Digital nomad experience: Four or more years.

Has lived/worked/travelled in: Dominica, Spain, and Trinidad & Tobago.

Normally stays in a country/city for: A month or so.

Makes a living as a: Freelance software manager, writer, translator, bits and bobs.

Meet Ivy

I was a full-time remote software implementation manager for nine years, before leaving my permanent position last summer to focus on my great creative passion, writing. I'm now a true freelancer — translating Spanish documents, caring for pets and children, publishing my creative writing pieces.

How Ivy got started

For nine years, I worked at a small tech company. When I started there in 2012, working from home was an almost unheard-of benefit, an unimaginable freedom that they offered. I was not enjoying one particularly harsh New York winter, clacking away on my computer in snowy isolation on my couch, when I thought, 'If I can work from home in Brooklyn, why can't I work from home in the Caribbean?'

I had just returned from an extended vacation on the tiny green-and-black (jungle-and-volcano) island of Dominica. Resorts and the trappings of the tourism industry had always made my stomach turn, so I'd stayed with a dear friend in an everyday sort of neighbourhood on the outskirts of Roseau, the capital. Neighbours were so friendly, the island so safe for a single woman, the food so savoury, I really felt like I could live a life there. For the benefit of my division's director, I cooked up elaborate, persuasive arguments for working abroad, and scheduled a meeting. The arguments weren't necessary. After my first sentence, the director interrupted: 'So you're saying you want to go to the Caribbean for the winter? Fine. Send me a postcard.'

So I spent the first winter in Dominica, and what can I say, it was the whole dream come true. Since visitor visas don't last forever, I started imagining all the places I could go. Until the pandemic hit, my life was a patchwork of times and places: three months *bodega*-hopping and beach-bumming in Andalucia, two months exploring ruined Jesuit cathedrals and Guarani rock paintings in Paraguay, a month hiking Taiwanese jungles and so on. The time difference with New York only helped; I realized how counterproductive a 9-to-5 job is for me. Much better to wake up, spend physical energy on getting to know a new place, and then settle in to work in the afternoon — less rush, less stress, more energy for what I really wanted to do.

And then, in March 2020, travel stopped. I traded in my sexy bachelorette status for a sweet, dependable man from the Midwest. A venture capital firm bought out the tech company and things went rapidly south (i.e. chokingly corporatized), so I left last summer, and have since been focusing on the great love of my life: creative writing.

Ivy's 'typical day'

The wanderlust didn't die when I left my job and regular paycheck — and gained a partner. I've just adjusted the durations of my trips to weeks instead of months, and now I travel with a purpose beyond pure enjoyment (although I maintain pure enjoyment is a 100 per cent valid reason to do anything). My trips now centre around advancing my encore career as an emerging writer. I attend writers' conferences and workshops taught by writers I admire, and I accept every invitation to read my work. The destinations — Albuquerque, Syracuse, rural Wisconsin — aren't found in travel brochures but they inspire more intense writing. My writing teacher, Natalie Goldberg, once said, 'Grey is good. Within bland is discovery. Go inside and find something.' The less-obviously exciting places allow me to continue the practices that support me as an artist without distraction.

Outside of the writing-related events themselves, a typical day on the road often looks much like it does at home: a long session of yoga stretches for my complaining hip, a trip to a gem of a farmers' market followed by some cooking therapy, finding a community park to write or rewrite a piece. Over the years, my travels have become much more 'people-centric'. I don't just want to see a place with my eyes and take in its balmy breezes; I want to connect with people who call it home. So I listen with great fascination while the mycologist at the farmers' market explains how he grew his blue oysters. I ask questions of the local poet who opened the reading for coffee. By the third time I pop into the same art gallery, I offer up an extra set of hands to the friendly gallery assistant sorting a mountain of promotional brochures. In a somewhat contracted world, this has become my new 'nomading': less isolated, more local. Going inside grey and finding something.

Ivy's favourite thing about the 'digital nomad' life is ...

The zest I wake up with every day, knowing something surprising and novel will happen.

Her least favourite thing about the 'digital nomad' life is ...

The loneliness. While the digital nomad life means you're meeting interesting new people all the time, nothing substitutes for your core friends and family — and this life means there's no such thing as just popping in on each other to cheer each other up when you've had a bad day.

The number one thing Ivy wished she knew when she first started out as a digital nomad is ...

Keep your commitments light. The magic of this lifestyle is that you can allow spontaneous experiences to come and sweep you up — and teach you things you never would've learned at home. If you overplan and book up all your days months ahead, you're beholden to experiences that haven't happened yet, over the current experience opening its arms to you at this moment.

14

Home:

Long-term travel changes your relationship with who you are

~~

When New Zealand slammed its borders shut in 2020, it seemed like just another cow swirling overhead in the crazy tornado that was our world back then. But through the start of 2022, when it was virtually impossible for even a citizen to return home, especially when travelling with a non-Kiwi partner, the idea of 'home' took on a strange resonance. Is it home, after all, if they won't let you in?

People will be debating the merits and proportionality of New Zealand's border closure for years and, as I've noticed from conversations with many from both sides, the position you take likely depends on whether you happened to be in the 'team of five million' (i.e. New Zealanders in New Zealand), or the 'team of one million' (i.e. Kiwis overseas). For those of us in the second category, there were many months at a time when, due to New Zealand's strictly enforced and highly limited military-run quarantine facilities, it was literally impossible for us to return home.

This was a strange thing to get your head around. Imagine you went out for a walk one day and, when you came home, you found your keys didn't fit the lock. You bang on the door. Your family is inside. You see them through the window. You hear their voices. They can hear you knock. But they shrug. You're stuck outside. They don't want you. Is this still your home?

Friends overseas were appalled by the border closure, and I watched the opinion of New Zealand plummet in the eyes of Poles, the British, Americans and even Ukranians I knew and associated with. And I've wrestled for a while with the implications of this. I still introduce myself as a Kiwi, travel on my New Zealand passport, and maintain it as my centre of vital interests. But I have also experienced being banned from its shores. How can one reconcile a home in which one is not welcome? Surely the words 'home' and 'welcome' belong together, as portrayed in the song 'Welcome Home' by the New Zealand musician Dave Dobbyn?

For many long-term travellers, a sense of not quite belonging is what propels us out the door in the first place. When I speak to friends of mine who travel for long periods of time, the anecdotal evidence seems to show higher than normal rates of divorced parents: the family home no longer exists.

I can remember the strange sense I felt when I moved out at seventeen after finishing high school to travel first around Australia and then around Europe. My mum had also moved out to build a new home with her partner, taking my younger sister with her. And so the home in which I grew up was gone. I was uprooted by choice, but untethered by circumstance. There was no familiar 'home' to return to, and so I built new homes around me.

Building a new home at short notice

You'll read in many of the nomad interviews that 'loneliness' on the road is unexpectedly rare. Travellers seek each other out on Facebook groups, couchsurfing meetups and in backpacker bars. In these places, it's natural to show up alone, introduce yourself, answer the ubiquitous 'Where are you from?' question, and end up with a travelling companion for your next adventure.

When I arrive somewhere new with the intention of living there, I typically try to do the following:

» Tap my personal network for an intro to anyone local. Chances are, a friend's sister's boyfriend will know someone in Istanbul or Tbilisi. Locals will often jump at the chance to hang out with a stranger from far away, and this can be an instant 'in'.

» Look up expat groups on Facebook. Search city of your choice plus 'expats'. No matter how small the town, you're likely to find a community of expats filling Facebook with posts about mobile phone plans, annoying construction works, a new sushi restaurant, and all sorts of trivia. Sometimes these forums can be supportive, positive places. Others can have a bit of a nastier culture. In either case, they are likely to contain useful information and maybe host meetup events where you can meet like-minded people. Increasingly, 'digital nomad' groups are worth looking into as well (see Chapter 4 on networking). While we don't travel simply to hang out with people from back home, a support group can help you find your feet and also result in other introductions. Don't hesitate to even look up 'British in ...', 'Americans in ...', 'Nozzies (New Zealanders and Aussies) in ...' groups. You'll eventually want to expand your circle beyond these groups, but they can be a gentle starting point, particularly if you are setting up somewhere exotic for the first time.

» Reach out to an interesting writer or journalist. I have this as my advantage as the editor of a travel-writing platform, but expat writers living in non-tourist towns can be very generous with their time. You may find yourself, as I have on happy occasions, listening to stories about encounters with presidents and prime ministers, first-hand accounts of Colour-Revolutions, and introductions to local wine makers.

» Say 'yes'. A spontaneous invite to coffee. An invitation to share dinner with a family. These things happen when you travel. While sometimes there can be malicious intentions behind these invitations (lads, if a suspiciously beautiful woman walks up to you on the street of a developing country and invites you to a bar, be careful!), most are genuinely well-meaning. For some analysis and advice on how to choose when to say yes and also facilitate more of these interactions, see my last book, *Travel Your Way: Rediscover the world on your own terms*.

Following these steps you'll gradually start feeling not so much like an interloper, but more like some kind of quasi-local. You'll pick up enough of the local language to order a beer in your regular watering hole. You'll have a local SIM card and regular weekly meetings with an international group of friends. You'll know the coffee shops that have stable Wi-Fi, and the bakeries where you can get a good deal on a Sunday afternoon. You'll walk the streets without having to look at Google Maps, making friendly eye contact with the old woman who is always out sweeping the streets. You'll even start to get acquainted with the stray cats who mew around the local rubbish bins. And then you may be wondering ... is this still travel?

For some, this heralds the transition from nomad to expat. For others, it's a signal that it's time to fire up Skyscanner and plan your next adventure. Many nomads end up creating real 'homes' away from the place where they grew up, and feeling just as connected to those lands as the place of their birth. I have felt this way about Poland, where my wife is from, and know many travellers who have similar experiences. Being sensitive to how your own identity is shifting as you travel and live away is one of the great joys, and also challenges, of the nomad life. And it really does make returning to your original 'home' a strange and unsettling experience. You simply cannot travel this long and this consistently without shifting your relationship with the world and yourself. Being open to the idea that even your sense of 'where home is' might shift is a scary thought, but something you may come to embrace as the months on the road stretch eventually into years.

Conclusion:
Your nomad transition plan

~~~

So let's bring it all together. Say you're currently not a digital nomad but you want to become one. Here are some ways that you could pull this off, depending on your current circumstances.

Case study: The office worker going remote

You like your job. Or maybe you don't like it, but it challenges you just enough that you're not dying of boredom while leaving your batteries charged enough to seek out adventure elsewhere. Your bills are covered, and if you took your current paycheck to cheaper parts of the world, you know your dollar could go even further. While you've flirted with the idea of going freelance or branching out and starting your own business, you aren't quite ready to give up the security of that corporate paycheck — especially if you don't have to.

You probably went fully remote during COVID-19 but now you are expected to come into the office once or twice per week. Your company is still figuring it out, but you're confident that you can still do your job 100 per cent online while exploring the sunny shores of Greece ... or maybe between tango lessons in Argentina. Let's put together a plan of action that could help you make the switch.

1. Start small. Going from being accessible in the office to being in a different time zone halfway across the world is a big leap. Instead, start small. Try to stick with the same time zone, and make a specific request for a fixed time period. If you're in the UK, start with two weeks working remotely in Greece before booking those flights to Argentina.

2. Deliver. Don't give your colleagues the impression that remote work is damaging your productivity. When you're on your initial work trips, make sure you deliver. Log in on time, smash your deadlines and make your work noticeable.

3. Limit bragging. Especially if you have work colleagues following you on socials, turn it down a little with the beachside pics. You don't want to give the impression that you're on holiday.

4. Make it a positive. I recently had a company I work for mention the fact that 'Nathan is always in a different country every time we

speak to him on Zoom' as a positive example of how open-minded and embracing their work culture is. And it's true! If you can praise your employer for 'allowing you to flourish in new ways and bring an extra dose of creativity to your work', you can convince them to see your remote escapades as advantageous for your work, rather than a distraction from it.

Once you have your company understanding that you working remotely costs them nothing and maybe even benefits them in the form of your loyalty and their image, then people may eventually stop asking where you are in any spirit except open curiosity. This has been my own experience, and those of others I've spoken with for this book. Of course, all companies vary and some corporations have more rigid cultures than others. Test the waters, take things step by step, and assess as you go.

Case study: The creative becoming freelance

You have always been sure about a particular talent you have, whether it's writing, designing, drawing, creating music or recording voice-overs. You know there's a market out there for people who can deliver with such skills, but so far this hasn't been your main source of income. It may not even have been something you've tried to make a living at in the past. Or, if it has, you've done so in a corporate context and you're keen to get out of it. Your goal is to transition out of your day job and set yourself up as a freelancer using your creative talent to facilitate your travels. Here are some tips to make that happen.

1. Start before you quit. While telling your boss to go take a hike and hurling your company laptop into the nearest lake may be a Monday afternoon fantasy, it's seldom the most prudent strategy! Instead, eke out whatever time you can to start hustling on the side (see 'side hustles' in Chapter 8 page 115). When your colleagues are goofing off on a slow day watching YouTube videos, you could be ... building your own portfolio website, making a list of potential clients, building your actual portfolio by creating demo projects, asking other people you know in this space if they are overworked and need someone to help with the spillover.

2. Cultivate connections. Freelancers work alone, but not really for themselves. As we explored in chapters 4 and 5, you gotta serve somebody. Share examples of your writing or art or voice-over work on LinkedIn and let people know you're looking for clients. When your day-job colleagues ask you about it, explain that it's a side hustle you're working on in your spare time.

3. Grind until you hit the tipping point. There's going to be a point when you have enough freelance work to say goodbye to the day job and focus fully on your freelance career. When this occurs is quite delicate. In the past I've 'downsized' full-time jobs for part-time consulting/freelance gigs to make the transition less painful. Sometimes, this means you get the best of both worlds: the freedom of a freelance career bolstered by a regular-corporate check. Other

times I've felt like it's the worst of both: the corporate grind without the benefits or compensation. Choose your moment based on your own risk tolerance. If you need motivation, ask yourself where you really want to be in five years, and which course of action you'd be least likely to regret in your old age.

A coda on entrepreneurship

The advice above for full-time workers who want to transition to being freelance also applies if you have a job but you'd prefer to be running a business. There's one more thing to add to that which is the subject of risk tolerance. So much 'digital nomad' advice already available basically says 'start a successful business' and I've tried hard to avoid echoing that here.

The fact is, owning a successful business requires a huge amount of grit, hard work, risk tolerance and yes, luck, and probably access to capital to kick it off. This is why I discuss in the 'side hustle' section of Chapter 8 the value of taking the gradual route, and building something additional to your day job. But that's not the only approach.

Enrique Hygge and others you've met in these pages gambled everything on their first business, often borrowing money from family and living off scraps for years before their businesses took off. Travelling can actually help, not hinder this.

If you're from the United States or New Zealand, for example, you may find the cost of living in somewhere like Eastern Europe or South-East Asia significantly less. This can reduce the day-to-day pressures and make it more realistic for you to take a gamble and invest significant amounts of your income, say from your remote job or freelance hobby, into your business idea.

Moving away can also be quite psychologically liberating, breaking the emotional patterns that might have stopped you from taking risks, and putting the chances of failure outside your immediate vision or judgment of friends and family, well-meaning though they probably are. It's a chance to do and see things differently than how you normally would. And being somewhere exotic makes everything a lot more fun.

Many years ago, a friend and I tried and failed to start a business in Shanghai. The business flopped but we had an enormous amount of fun brainstorming until late at night in an exotic part of the world. And the ideas we generated during that period — about copywriting, ecommerce and expat life in general — have made appearances in our subsequent careers as we straddled the lines between employee, freelancer and business owner. If you're in a position where you have no dependents and you can live cheaply for a while, then taking the risk and going all in could make sense. And, if not, I suggest you go with the incremental side hustle approach advocated in the freelance case study and in the Entrepreneurship chapter. Either way, you'll ensure that you're spending at least some of your work hours building something that matters to you.

Case study: Students and first-time job seekers

I ran my first business while I was still a university student. Taking a cushy arts degree gave me plenty of time to figure out the then still fairly new worlds of blogging and internet marketing. Selling ebooks and online courses made me enough to pay off the uni fees and get me around Europe and into China. When the money I made from selling the small business ran out, I made an assessment of my skills, and found I knew about writing and selling things online. I put the word out to my network that I was a freelance copywriter specializing in websites, and the journey began.

Many degrees, especially the more expensive and vocational ones, are designed to corral you into a fixed career path. And if you have a hefty student loan hanging over your head, the idea of spending money on travel can seem unrealistic. But I hope this book has made clear that travelling does not mean you need to sacrifice your career growth, your productivity or your creativity. And given that much of the world is probably cheaper to live in than where you come from, it doesn't mean you need to be spending more either.

When taking your first steps into the workforce, consider seeking out companies that offer generous remote-working terms. Websites like Flexjobs.com and Remote.co specifically curate remote offers. You could also use your student status as an advantage, and take a semester abroad somewhere exotic (I chose China) and use that as an opportunity to make local connections who could help you branch out into a business or freelance career.

Your options are open

Both the techniques and the experience of being a digital nomad in today's world require adaptability and creativity. Getting established can take time, and life on the road is not all beachside cocktails and exotic adventures. You're going to have to work a lot, and balance almost all of the bullshit demands of regular existence on Planet Earth with the challenges of surviving in unfamiliar cultures, often with no support systems and where you don't even speak the language. To get paid by people who could easily hire someone who does not disappear on eighteen-hour train rides or flood their social media with snaps from bars in random Asian cities, you're going to have to be better than most at your chosen craft. To stay sane amid the loneliness, chaos or confusion you may feel while on the road, you're going to need to constantly remind yourself why you're doing it. No matter what you're working at now, if you have a skill, reasonable organizational abilities and the power to adapt to changing circumstances, then the digital nomad life (or whatever you want to call it!) is within reach. Make a plan. Book a flight. And get ready for an adventure.

Resources

~~~

Financing/Banking

Here are some options for nomad-friendly bank accounts that are designed for people to earn and spend in multiple currencies.

Wise.com

N26.com

Revolut.com

Mobile phone and eSim

How to stay connected and avoid roaming fees without having to fumble around with local SIM cards.

Aairalo.com

https://redteago.com/

Insurance

Here are some travel insurance options created with digital nomads in mind.

SafetyWing.com
WorldNomads.com

Accommodation

These commonly used accommodation search engines have been employed by digital nomads to form connections with landlords who may be able to offer longer-term options.

Airbnb.com

Booking.com

Freelance platforms

While these platforms have their flaws, many freelancers find them a useful place for beginning their careers and making initial client connections.

Freelancer.com

Fiverr.com

Indeed

Glassdoor

Findstack.com

Remote job listings

For those seeking more permanent, stable employment that you can nevertheless take with you on the road, these places may provide some options.

Remote.co

Flexjobs.com

These platforms connect Western teachers to students in places like China.

VIPkid.com

Magic Ears (https://t.mmears.com/v2/)

https://teacher.qkids.com

https://www.onlineenglishteaching.com/say-abc

https://www.saporedicina.com/english/teach-english-online-to-chinese-kids/

Getting there

Air flights

SkyScanner.net

Google Flights

RyanAir

AirAsia

Ride sharing

FlixBus (ride sharing)

BlaBlaCar (ride sharing, especially in Europe)

Train travel

bahn.com/en (book internationally anywhere in Europe)

Networking

Travelling can be lonely. Whether you're looking for clients or friends, these platforms can help you form a local community.

Facebook.com: Search 'Expats in [insert city]'

LinkedIn.com: Update your location to be found by local employers

MeetUp.com

CouchSurfing.com

Index

INDEX

Flexijobs.com 212
FlixBus 126
flying 125–26, 149, 155–56
France 26, 71, 72, 108, 109, 153, 181, 183, 184, 188
freedom 9, 11, 14, 15, 21, 40, 54, 72, 73, 89, 91, 110, 117, 157, 172, 179, 185, 195, 208
Freelancer 116
freelancing 20, 44, 55, 58, 66–68, 71, 94, 101, 115, 153, 170, 194
  see also side hustle
  combining with part-time employment 104, 208–09
  coping when things go wrong 68–70
  defining a niche 80–81, 82, 85, 86
  five broad types 44–50
  platforms 216
  transition plan for a creative going freelance 207–09

G
geo-arbitrage 111, 188, 189–90
Georgia 131, 132, 150–51, 176–79, 188, 190, 191
Germany 119, 121, 129, 188
Ghana 38
gigs 58, 68, 78, 94, 155, 208
Glassdoor 94
GoDaddy 116
Goldberg, Natalie 197
Google Flights 126
Google Voice 129
graphic design 46, 63, 64
Greece 26, 108, 188
Grenada 26

H
health insurance 54, 127, 132
health issues 127, 131
home, creating in new places 176–77, 202–04
homestays 156
Hong Kong 153, 187
hostels 156, 188
hotels 156, 180
hours of work 39, 49, 50, 53, 91–92, 98, 101, 102, 117, 136, 152
house-sitting 71, 72
Hungary 191
hustle culture 32, 85
  see also side hustle
hybrid work 102, 103, 105
Hygge, Enrique 23, 97–99, 117, 209

I
Iceland 71, 72, 187

incomes 33, 55, 59, 60, 61, 91–92, 102, 124–25
  see also expenses; invoices; pricing
  fluctuations 54, 73–74
Indeed.com 94, 104
India 135, 136, 154, 156, 181–82, 187
Indonesia 26, 71, 153, 187
inflation 123–24
Instagram 22, 32, 38, 99
insurance 54, 127, 132, 216
internet connection *see* VPN (virtual private network); Wi-Fi
Intrepid Times 52, 116–18
invoices 58, 59, 63, 68–69
Iraq 170, 187
Ireland 26
Italy 153, 188, 191

J
Jamaica 108, 188
job listings 217
job seekers, first-time 211–12
Jordan 170, 188
journalism 24, 155, 170, 183, 184, 203
journalling 181, 185

K
Kazakhstan 121, 166
Kirkham, Barrington (Barry) 22–23, 87–89
Kyrgyzstan 170, 171, 188

L
languages 34, 50, 119, 120, 121, 148, 149, 157, 176, 181, 184, 185, 203, 212
Laos 153, 188
libraries as workplaces 98
life-long nomads 33
LinkedIn 64–65, 76, 79, 82–83, 103, 208
loneliness 102, 109, 173, 198, 201–02, 212, 218
Los Angeles 71, 72
lovagobondo.com 153

M
Malaysia 153, 188
Malta 108, 188
marketing 10, 19, 47, 50, 75, 87, 88, 116, 154, 155, 156, 160, 211
media organizations 77
Medium 79
meetups 65–66, 85–86, 102, 201, 202
Mexico 26, 71, 110, 187
mobile phones
  resources 215
  roaming fees 128, 149
  work notifications 150, 151
Montserrat 129